Teaching Notes on Piano Exam Pieces 2009–2010

Grades 1–7

TIMOTHY BARRATT

JULIAN HELLABY

VANESSA LATARCHE

MARGARET MURRAY McLEOD

ANTHONY WILLIAMS

Teaching Notes on Piano Exam Pieces 2009–2010

Grades 1–7

With an introduction by CLARA TAYLOR, Chief Examiner of
The Associated Board of the Royal Schools of Music

The Associated Board of the Royal Schools of Music

First published in 2008 by
The Associated Board of the Royal Schools of Music (Publishing) Limited
24 Portland Place, London W1B 1LU, United Kingdom

© 2008 by The Associated Board of the Royal Schools of Music

ISBN: 978 1 86096 739 9

AB 3410

A CIP catalogue for this book is available from The British Library.

Typeset by Hope Services (Abingdon) Ltd
Printed in England by Martins the Printers Limited, Berwick-upon-Tweed

CONTENTS

NOTES ON CONTRIBUTORS

Timothy Barratt, ARAM GRSM LRAM ARCM LMusTCL, is a professor at the Royal Academy of Music and Head of Keyboard at Dulwich College, London. He has toured extensively and broadcast as a solo pianist, accompanist and chamber music player. He adjudicates, directs workshops for teachers and is an Associated Board examiner, trainer and consultant moderator, and a mentor for the Board's Certificate of Teaching.

Julian Hellaby, PhD MMus BMus LRAM ARAM, studied piano at the Royal Academy of Music and has performed throughout the UK and overseas. He is an Associated Board examiner, trainer, moderator and public presenter, as well as a mentor for the Board's Certificate of Teaching course. He has extensive experience of piano teaching at all levels, and is currently Associate Senior Lecturer at Coventry University. He recently released his sixth CD, a recording of Russian piano music.

Vanessa Latarche, Hon ARAM FTCL LRAM ARCM, has established a reputation as a leading teacher. She is Head of Keyboard at the Royal College of Music, London and an Associated Board moderator, trainer, examiner and presenter, working internationally in most capacities. As a performer she enjoys a busy concert schedule and gives broadcasts for the BBC. She is also an experienced adjudicator and gives masterclasses in the UK and abroad.

Margaret Murray McLeod, ARAM FTCL LRAM ARCM, studied piano and composition at the Royal Academy of Music. As well as performing as a soloist and accompanist, she has many years' experience of teaching at all levels. From 1972 she trained student teachers and performers at Napier University, Edinburgh, where she was Senior Lecturer for Performance Studies until 1997. Her work as a lecturer, examiner and adjudicator has taken her worldwide.

Anthony Williams, MMus Dip.RAM GRSM LRAM, has an active performing, teaching and adjudicating career in the UK and abroad and is currently Head of Keyboard and Instrumental Music at Radley College, Oxfordshire. He is an examiner (jazz and classical), trainer and moderator for the Associated Board as well as a mentor for its Certificate of Teaching. He is the co-author of previous *Teaching Notes*, with Clara Taylor, and the compiler of *Fingerprints* (Faber, 2002), a collection of original repertoire for piano teaching.

NOTES ON CONTRIBUTORS

INTRODUCTION

Teachers always enjoy sharing professional insights. The contributors to these *Teaching Notes* – all distinguished teachers as well as being examiners – are no exception. Their enthusiasm shines out of the text and I know they have relished the detailed investigation into this exciting new syllabus. Writing commentaries is, of course, a very time-consuming exercise and regretfully it is no longer possible for me to be a regular contributor with the ever-increasing demands of the Associated Board's new initiatives. However, I am retaining a close interest and connection with these notes and take pleasure in providing the introduction.

The wide choice of repertoire for every grade gives the opportunity to match the pieces to the pupil. Sometimes you might choose a style that immediately suits, and at other times you might take a more medicinal approach in order to tackle shortcomings. There are obvious winners on the lists, which will appear many times in the exams, but do also explore the alternative pieces not published in the graded volumes. There are some delights to be found that may just be the answer for some pupils. The inclusion of a few arrangements marks a new departure for the piano syllabus. We hope this will be beneficial in widening repertoire choices at the lower grades, and more importantly introduce young pianists to, and encourage their interest in, the wider world of other non-pianistic genres.

From Grade 1 to Grade 8 the three lists have more in common than you might expect. List A contains the technically demanding repertoire, List B the more warmly expressive pieces, and List C has a tremendous variety of styles, often with some jazzy rhythms. Despite the enormous difference in standards between Grade 1 and Grade 8, candidates' strengths and weaknesses tend to follow predictable paths in each list. I believe it will be helpful, therefore, to consider the three lists in more detail.

LIST A

In List A, definition of fingerwork, clarity of articulation and control of co-ordination are necessary, as fluency increases through the grades. These technical challenges, especially runs and ornaments, can upset the basic rhythm, and in their determination some candidates use an over-emphatic heavy touch that is self-defeating. An ability to keep the hands in exact ensemble is needed. Examiners often hear hands starting together then parting company at difficult corners. In higher grades, part-playing will often be a feature in List A and it's fairly rare to hear this successfully achieved. Many candidates over-emphasize the subject without adjusting the balance of the other lines. When this happens, control of dynamics and phrasing is inevitably affected.

Ornaments can be simplified or omitted in the early grades if they are causing problems with the rhythm. A steady basic beat is a higher priority than the decorations. In later grades some ornamentation is often necessary and certainly needs to be included to achieve higher marks.

In their efforts to manage the technicalities, many candidates are less aware of the musical content of the List A pieces. It's a delight to hear the right texture, clear dynamics and musical phrasing capturing the elegant style of the repertoire, which often comes from quite an early era.

LIST B

List B gives every opportunity to show more expressive phrasing and tonal warmth. The pieces are selected mostly from the Classical or Romantic styles, and cantabile tone will be needed for the melodies. Phrasing comes right to the forefront and balance of hands needs real care, as these pieces often follow the pattern of right-hand melody and left-hand accompaniment. Pedalling will be necessary for the more legato choices, with clean, rhythmic legato pedalling requiring good physical co-ordination. Even in higher grades we frequently hear the hands and the right foot not really coinciding.

Rubato is a vital part of musical phrasing and is often needed in the List B pieces. Candidates are usually better at slowing down than getting faster, so it will be helpful to explain the concept of a balanced rubato during the practice period.

Dynamics tend to be more smoothly graded in the styles chosen for this list, and ability to mould the tone evenly in each hand is something to aim for at all stages. Subtlety of tone colour and control of rubato within the stylistic discipline of the pieces are high priorities. Often the pieces have descriptive titles, giving a clue to the mood and atmosphere of the music.

LIST C

This list offers something for everyone. These days there is tremendous variety – jazz pieces, contemporary items and a host of other styles – which should make it easy to find exactly the right choice for your pupils.

In the early grades the jazz items are always hugely popular. Candidates can manage quite difficult rhythms when they like the music. Strongly rhythmic, dynamic pieces, such as the all-time hit *The Swinging Sioux* from the 1999–2000 Grade 1 syllabus, seem to capture the imagination of thousands of candidates throughout the world.

With such variety on offer, it's important to go to the heart of what each piece really requires to make an effective performance. Very often this means having a feel for the underlying beat, which will be more pronounced in the jazz pieces but still vital in many contemporary items. Colourful playing, evoking the various moods and sound worlds, will be enjoyable to explore, and candidates often feel they can relax and communicate these pieces, achieving more of a sense of performance than they manage with pieces from either of the two other lists.

Swung rhythm is an issue right from Grade 1. This is not the place to give a detailed description (which really needs a demonstration to make the point), but it will help pupils to imagine that 4/4 time becomes 12/8, so that a dotted-quaver, semiquaver rhythm sounds more like crotchet, quaver. Pupils often catch on to this in certain parts of the piece, but find it difficult to be consistent, therefore causing the examiner to comment: 'Try to keep an even rhythm.' This does not mean that the swung rhythm has not been noticed, but usually indicates that there's an inconsistency in managing this throughout the performance. It is also perfectly acceptable to play the piece 'straight', especially in the lower grades, as long as the mood and relaxed feel of this style still come across. In the higher grades, the jazz pieces are quite sophisticated and often need a sense of swing and appreciation of whichever jazz style is appropriate to the piece.

In List C the metronome mark is often the composer's, so it pays to take notice and check carefully; as in Lists A and B, a metronome mark in square brackets indicates that it is an editorial suggestion, allowing a little more freedom of choice.

Young pupils often have a refreshingly open mind about contemporary items. Teachers may find some of the pieces slightly off-putting, but may be surprised to find that their students can get inside the music quite quickly and thoroughly enjoy playing in a different idiom.

Candidates are free to choose the order of their three pieces. It may well be wise to put the more technically demanding List A piece somewhere other than first in the exam. Many pupils these days start with their favourite piece, which helps their confidence when they come to tackle the others. It is sometimes rather disappointingly obvious why a piece has been left until last!

The extensive selection for each grade should ensure that each one of your candidates is happy and comfortable with the choice and order of his or her pieces. As teachers will be well aware, the candidate's attitude of mind as he or she enters the exam room is inevitably reflected in the result.

If you have any queries arising from this publication, do not hesitate to contact me, preferably by email (chiefexaminer@abrsm.ac.uk).

All good wishes to users of these notes, who will be inspired and reassured as the excellent selection of pieces becomes the graded pianistic diet for the coming exam sessions.

Clara Taylor

GRADE 1

Pupils will usually have been learning for up to eighteen months by the time Grade 1 is on the horizon. They may have taken the Prep Test during this time, in which case they will probably feel quite confident when facing this first real exam. A wide choice of pieces should help to keep motivation high, so why not have some alternatives prepared, then choose the best three as the exam approaches? The criteria for assessment for all grades are printed in *These Music Exams* – a useful source of reference for teachers.

A:1 Duncombe *Gavot*

The attractive appeal of this Gavot, which was composed by an English contemporary of Bach and Handel, lies in its simple texture and gently shaped melodic line. The absence of black notes will be welcomed, and there are few danger spots in the note sequences.

The piece appears designed to develop clarity and evenness in the fingers. Keeping the pulse steady when switching between quavers and triplets is a challenge in the outer sections; a feel for these changes in pattern can be developed, either by inventing words to fit the rhythms or clapping/singing alternate groups while maintaining a crotchet pulse. Confident, clean fingerwork with no overlap of sounds will be required, and despite the dynamic level of *forte*, a dance-like 'spring' can be given to the rhythm by detaching the crotchets and lightening second beats. In bars 7 and 23, slurring the quavers in pairs (releasing the second note) will allow the chords that follow to be placed confidently.

A softer tone and long lines provide contrast for the middle section. Careful fingering will ensure legato (the left-hand thumb may need particular attention), and the right hand's two-bar sequences can be enhanced by a gentle rise and fall in tone. Isolated practice will be needed to co-ordinate the legato and staccato in bar 16 before achieving a seamless join into bar 17; a crescendo will herald the final *forte*.

A:2 Kirnberger *Minuetto*

No syllabus seems complete without at least one Minuet in its list! Here is a piece that is elegant and charming in addition to being relatively unknown.

A good sense of keyboard geography is essential, as a fair amount of movement in both hands needs to be negotiated without any interruption in flow. Octave leaps in the left hand should be identified, and watch out for the change of finger on the repeated right-hand notes in bar 11. The trills (turns, in effect) at the end of each section must be fitted into the crotchet pulse; it is always safer, however, to omit them at this grade if they prove troublesome.

Observing the detailed right-hand phrasing will help to capture the gracefulness of this eighteenth-century dance. Quaver slurs need sensitive shaping in order not to clip the second note, and unslurred notes may be detached. Lightly detaching most left-hand crotchets will give definition to the bass line, as if played on the cello. Practising scales or five-finger exercises, both staccato and slurred in pairs, may prove useful.

Forte indicates a bright, confident sound, which should never be heavy, especially on second and third beats. Smoother phrasing provides contrast at bars 9–12, and a clear drop to *piano* will allow the crescendo to project effectively.

A:3 Vivaldi *L'autunno (Autumn)*

How satisfying it is for pianists to get their hands on familiar music normally played by orchestras throughout the world! The arrangement of this attractive piece lies well under the fingers, making it a real joy to learn and perform.

Clear dynamic contrasts every four bars highlight the echo effects that are such a familiar feature of the Baroque style. The left hand (the notes of which lie within a five-finger position, apart from the stretch for the third finger in bars 3 and 7) should always accompany, never overpower, the right. A sprightly one-in-a-bar feel can be achieved at the beginning and the end by slurring the right-hand dotted figures (stretch permitting) and keeping the second and third beats light and detached. Dotted quavers should be given their full length for the rhythm to remain taut; treating the semiquavers as grace notes preceding the following beat might help to keep them sufficiently short.

There must be no pulse distortion when the right hand shifts up the octave and back (bars 14–18). In these *forte* thirds the brilliance of two violins can be imitated; a good hand position, with all fingers curved, will ensure that both right-hand notes sound exactly together. Remember that the echo down the octave needs to start precisely where indicated, and bars that contain only one chord must be held for their full value.

6

A:4 Gläser *Angloise*

This attractive and cheerful piece by a little-known contemporary of Haydn and Mozart may serve as a good introduction to the Classical period. A stylish performance of it will depend on clear rhythm and sprightly phrasing.

Setting a maintainable tempo is one of the most important lessons for the aspiring pianist to learn and here the semiquaver groups should be used to indicate a manageable pace. Left-hand practice will enable the leaps to be negotiated reliably (confident thumb placing in bars 8, 14 and 16 is especially important), and bar 3 must be as nimbly executed as its neighbouring right-hand patterns. Starting the right hand of bar 2 and elsewhere on 3/1 would utilize the stronger fingers. If necessary the phrased couplets in bar 7 may be omitted and replaced with legato semiquavers. Take care not to lose momentum at the double bar midway.

Staccato 'wedges' indicated by the composer offer some clues as to articulation but elsewhere buoyancy will be given to the rhythm by detaching crotchets and quavers to contrast with smoother semiquavers. Dynamics are left to the player's imagination: a generally forthright tone with a drop in level at the start of the second half might be effective, but the lighter, more delicate tone of eighteenth-century instruments must always be considered.

A:5 Handel *March in G*

This March conveys a sense of majesty and importance through its strong rhythm and clear two-part texture. The speed of marching is stately rather than hurried (minim = 66–72), with two-in-a-bar being communicated by lightening the off-beats. Care should be taken not to shorten the long notes, especially at the end of the first half.

Baroque bass lines often leap around and this piece is no exception; special practice will be needed to develop left-hand confidence. There are no hard-and-fast rules regarding phrasing, but a stylish effect will be achieved if crotchets and minims are generally detached – with the exception of the crotchet, two-quaver patterns which may be slurred. Imagining the piece as a duet for violin and cello (or oboe and bassoon) might encourage the forthright approach needed. Although much of the piece can be strong-toned, some dynamic variety will help to maintain musical interest: consider either building a crescendo for the last four bars of each half or making echo effects at repeated bars. The imitation between the hands, which gives a conversational character to bars 11–14, needs clarity and careful rhythmic pacing. Any ritardando at the end should be made gradually, with the final note held for its full length.

A:6 Purcell *Minuet in A minor*

This is a beautiful Minuet; one which in sensitive hands can sound ravishing. When note-learning, the ternary structure – with the final eight bars an exact repeat of the opening section – is a real bonus. The right hand presents few problems, but the trill in bar 11, played as either eight semiquavers or six triplet quavers, must be integrated into the crotchet pulse. The two-part texture of the left hand will require good fingering to sustain the notes; although some compromise may be needed for small hands, the impression of two sustained bass 'voices' should be conveyed as much as possible.

The overall mood is one of measured gracefulness with a gentle one-in-a-bar feel. Dynamic levels are varied at each four-bar section, and a gentle rise and fall of tone within phrases, as if sung, will breathe life into the melodic line. Bars 9–12 form the central and strongest-toned section, but lightening the second and third beats here and elsewhere will help to create a sense of dance. Good hand and finger independence is needed in order to detach the unslurred right-hand crotchets of the opening while maintaining a smooth, quieter line in the left hand; players should avoid unwanted accents on staccato notes.

B:1 Dunhill *A Song of Erin*

The romantic and literary name for Ireland, 'Erin', is used here to suggest a peaceful folksong style. This well-crafted, accessible piece is suited to young players because it lies well under the hands. Any changes of left-hand position are preceded by rests (bars 7, 9, 12 and 15), and the right hand only diverges from its original position in the third line. The balance between the hands needs attention; the left hand should gently support rather than overpower the right-hand line.

Encourage a beautiful smooth singing tone for the right-hand melody, with a sweet gentle sound at the beginning. At first, sing with your pupils while they play the melody without the left hand. This will bring out the natural shaping – swelling up to the phrase's top note (e.g. the top C in bar 2) and decreasing the sound at the phrase-ending (e.g. in bar 4).

One of the most challenging issues for an inexperienced young player in performance is holding long notes. Bars 8 and 16 should initially be counted aloud, to ensure that the semibreves receive full value. Pupils can then be encouraged to listen to the sound of the note dying away, particularly in bar 16 after the expressive diminuendo and *poco rit.* Sitting still for this is helpful, and will ensure control at the end of the performance.

B:2 Gedike *Kummer (Grief)*

This is another cantabile piece for the B List which needs excellent expressive and rhythmic control. The chanting right-hand melody is initially unaccompanied, later becoming much more complex with the introduction of the delicious left-hand harmony from bar 9.

If the tempo is set too fast at the opening, the textural change in the third line may cause anxiety, leading inevitably to a change of pulse. Much time will be spent learning lines 3 and 4, therefore, before the piece can be played fluently at a suitable tempo. When at the performance stage, the player must think of the pulse of the third line before playing the very first note, in order to set the right tempo and mood.

The tempo marking of Adagio suggests a slow two-in-a-bar, so the quavers must not run out of control but be expressively legato; tenuto signs over the Es in bars 2 and 10 suggest dragging the changing fingers to imitate a child sobbing. The tenuto mark over the F in bar 3 also needs expressive emphasis as it is the loudest note of the first phrase. After much rise and fall in the phrasing, the melody passes to the left hand in bar 16. Hold back in tempo to observe the sostenuto, and enjoy the little glimpse of optimism offered by the sharpened 3rd in the final chord.

B:3 Trad. English *Early one morning*

This arrangement of the well-known traditional song opens with a slow and sleepy four-bar introduction in the left hand; this allows the young player to establish placement of the stretchy arpeggio figures before the right-hand melody joins in. Breathing in deeply during the crotchet rests of bars 2 and 4 (and out again on the first beats of the following bars) will aid the waking-up process and also keep the inexperienced player in control of the rhythm.

The opening melody in bar 5 will need a firm legato touch, and from the start of the learning process it will be essential to take care over fingering.

In addition, the ends of phrases in bars 8, 9 and 10 would benefit from lifting both hands gently; this not only gives space in the phrasing but also realigns the hands into position for the following phrase.

Dynamics are clearly marked by the arranger, but add extra interest through careful phrasing – for example, making little swells towards the middle of bars 9 and 10 (the latter bar presenting an opportunity for an echo). The final cadence needs placing, easing down over the last two quavers of the scale (second beat of bar 12) to end quietly, but also firmly enough for the last note to sing.

B:4 Dvořák *Cavatina*

As is typical of a Cavatina, this short song-like melody is full of serene charm and expression. Originally written for two violins and viola by the composer, it will suit a student who enjoys lyrical pieces.

One important detail to note is that the melody is sometimes divided between the hands; in bars 2, 4, 10 and 12 the last melodic note of each phrase is taken by the left hand. To avoid a bumpy line attention must be paid to the left-hand thumb, which should be played subtly at the end of each phrase. Practising the melody line alone without the other notes in the left-hand accompaniment will make the ear aware of the line. Another tricky part to voice is in bar 13, where the first note in the left hand (minim G) needs to connect smoothly up to the right-hand crotchet G on the third beat.

Dynamics do not raise much above *mezzo-forte* at the highest points of the crescendos, and the last chord, played very quietly, must be given its full value with the pause observed. Holding this last chord will need rehearsing, as the temptation for enthusiastic candidates to miscount and rush on to their next piece in the exam room can prove to be too much!

B:5 Marjorie Helyer *Dragonflies*

Imitating these swiftly-flying insects, the music darts around, demanding nimble fingers; the range of notes used is not wide, however, so it is an ideal piece for a student with small hands. Players will enjoy the lilting pulse and the textural clarity that can be achieved with light and even fingerwork. In bar 2 and similar the swirling sounds need upper-arm freedom for the line to be passed effortlessly between the hands. Gentle lifting of the hand at the ends of right-hand slurs in bars 2, 3, 4 etc. will add to the graceful feel.

Fingering is generally well-marked, but a couple of suggestions may ease the way. Firstly, it may be best to use finger 3 on the left-hand B in bar 6, then substitute with the thumb, leaving finger 2 to play B♭ in bar 7 and fingers 3 and 5 to play F and A in bar 8. Secondly, in bar 23, a thumb on the left-hand B♭, followed by finger 5 on C, leaves fingers 1 and 2 ready to play the final left-hand chord.

Dynamics are clear but the piece's overall shape will be particularly effective if the *forte* in bar 16 is reached after a well-graded crescendo. The quietest notes are the final ones where the jewel-coloured insects come to rest, or hover for a while.

B:6 Schubert *Theme from the 'Unfinished' Symphony*

Learning a simple piano arrangement of a well-known orchestral theme is an excellent way of introducing a famous work to the young musician. This has the bonus of being written in large and clear notation, and – some pupils may see this as an advantage – it contains only nine bars of music which are repeated to make the full page.

Originally stated in the symphony by the cellos, the main theme will need a good singing left hand. Playing your students an orchestral recording of the first movement of the symphony will give them an understanding of the orchestration and the sounds that they need to imitate. This will inspire them to practise projecting the left-hand melody as the cellists do, and to accompany sensitively with the right-hand chords, which should throb quietly in the background. Although it is relatively straightforward technically, in bar 2 and similar places with the dotted quaver, semiquaver rhythmic pattern, the co-ordination of the dotted rhythm in the left hand with the repeated quaver chords in the right is likely to be troublesome. Isolated and repeated practice of the first beat of the bar leading on to and stopping on the second beat will cure this if tackled from the outset.

Hours of fun are ahead here, guaranteed to have parents whistling the tune once fluency has been achieved.

C:1 Árpád Balázs *Trudging*

To create a characterful performance, it may be useful to visualize a weary traveller roaming across the countryside on horseback. 'Trudging' should be played at a steady tread, without any suggestion of a canter, never mind a gallop! In fact, no modification to the basic tempo is necessary other than an infinitesimal pause in bar 8 to reflect the 'comma'.

The music's trudging rhythmic character may be achieved by forearm movements: this can be practised initially by tapping on a flat surface, lifting the wrist a little after contact with the surface in readiness for the next relaxed descent. The same motion should then be transferred to the keyboard. The resulting slightly heavy, detached sound also fulfils the implications of the short horizontal lines below each quaver. Larger hands may like to finger the right-hand intervals in the first two bars with 5/2, 2/1, 3/1, and in bars 7–8 with 5/1, 2/1, 3/1, to minimize position changes.

The dynamic level remains largely *mezzo-forte*, but with an increased downward thrust of the forearm to achieve *sforzando* in bar 8. To gauge the final diminuendo, remember that bar 17 opens at *mezzo-forte* with the level reaching *piano* by bar 19. For the bored foot, *una corda* can be added at the very end – and remember to count carefully here, since the musical humour is lost if the quavers commence on the beat.

C:2 Paul Drayton *Never Vex a Tyrannosaurus Rex!*

By the sound of this piece, and despite the warning in its title, vexation seems to be exactly what is going on, ending in some kind of disaster – the nature of which is probably best left to your pupil's imagination!

One must assume that the T-Rex is getting gradually closer since the music opens *piano* and ends *fortissimo*, so this ominous crescendo needs to be strongly apparent to the examiner. It could be useful to practise just the first three notes at progressively louder volumes, gradually increasing the finger-lift and the amount of arm weight engaged. All the downward force your pupil can muster is required to play the last line; perhaps also consider allowing your pupil to use the side of a fist for the final note-cluster.

There are only four different right-hand chords: the learning process can be aided if pupils examine these in isolation, identifying which note has changed from one chord to the next. It will soon be apparent that very little hand movement is necessary. Where there are three chords in a row, a small lift of the arm between each and a slight separation of the one from its neighbour will help to project the accents.

The obvious pictorialism of this music is an attractive feature. It also offers an engaging introduction to the chromatic scale!

C:3 John Rowcroft *African Dance*

The South African 'Township' style is lively and exuberant but not too fast; note the 'relaxed' direction at the top. Nevertheless, rhythms need to be precise, with quavers played straight rather than swung.

The left-hand part poses some of the biggest challenges, so it may be advisable to work on this first. Mastery of the chord shapes can be achieved by building up the playing sensation, playing at first just two notes of the chord before adding the third. Memorization of these shapes in bars 1–4 will then allow your pupil to focus attention on the right hand. When working on the right-hand chords in bars 9–12, the hand will have to be held sufficiently forward to allow a smooth thumb passage from the B♭ to the A.

Articulations are clearly indicated but notes at phrase-mark endings, in places such as the second beat of bar 2, may be very slightly shortened to convey the melodic style of the piece. The chords in bars 11 and 15 can also be slightly separated, to highlight the syncopation. Other than *mezzo-forte* no dynamic is specified, but this sparsity need not be taken too literally. For example, colour and interest are added by introducing a diminuendo into bars 9 and 10, then a crescendo from the third beat of bar 13, reaching *forte* by the end. Happy jiving!

C:4 Chen Yi *Singing in the Mountain*

Children are often fascinated by the pedal, yet so little repertoire introduces it at an early learning stage – so here is a piece for the inquisitive foot! The effects are produced mainly through long, sustained sonorities, but in bar 11 there is one change that involves simple legato pedalling technique. This occurs around a long note, thus allowing plenty of time for depressing the pedal after lifting it with the change of bass notes.

The composer specifies that all treble-clef parts are to be played an octave higher than written, other than in bars 6, 12 and 13. To reach the high notes it is probably inadvisable to abandon a central sitting position, especially since lower notes also have to be played. Leaning over to the right and slightly backwards, remaining as relaxed as possible, will bring the notes within fairly easy reach.

The main melodic parts are all marked *forte*, yet the composer states that these moments should 'sing out from the top of the piano'. The *forte* should therefore be achieved by a deep, firm touch, with the necessary pressure achieved from well-raised fingers more than from forearm attack. The staccato notes may be helped by a gentle forearm drop and lift, producing a bell-like resonance.

This impressionistic music is likely to appeal to those with more sophisticated tastes and may be ideal for an adult learner.

C:5 Alan Haughton *Bluemerang*

This boogie-style piece is likely to have wide appeal and could be a popular choice. The style is probably best realized if the rhythms, despite their dotted appearance, are played swung and at a relaxed pace. A tempo range of crotchet = *c.*100 up to crotchet = *c.*108 will provide a suitably laid-back beat.

Rhythmic steadiness is essential, and relaxed, alternating hand/forearm movements may be rehearsed on a table-top to cultivate the necessary physical sensation. Syncopations in places such as bar 4 can be practised firstly by sounding the tied note on beat 3. Once the exact placement of the offbeat note has been grasped, the tie may be reintroduced and the rhythm simply 'felt'.

The examiner will want to hear effective contrast between the four dynamic levels marked. The hardest to differentiate will be *mezzo-piano* and *mezzo-forte*; these could be worked on first, with hands and fingers kept fairly close to the keys for the former and a little higher above for the latter. *Forte* and *piano* levels can then be organized accordingly. Testing these dynamics on the exam-room piano might be a good way to use the few moments of warm-up time before the exam starts.

If your pupil has access to an electric keyboard, practising this piece to a boogie backing may help to develop an appropriate sense of style – and would also be great fun!

C:6 Kabalevsky *My Stubborn Little Brother*

Younger brothers will no doubt have some sympathy with the stubborn character in this musical portrait. Imagine having to listen to all that nagging from the older sibling!

Musical dialogue is an important feature, and projection of the dynamics is essential to convey it. To achieve the necessary attack on the repeated D♭s, your pupil could try using the thumb, swinging it forcibly down from the wrist and forearm. In the last bar, jabbing from finger 3 will achieve an even more percussive effect (matching the *fortissimo*), and will bring the final chord within easy reach.

Short crescendos in places such as bar 10 will have to be very steep but, for maximum effect, most of the volume increase in the longer crescendos should be left to the second half of the bar. Pedalling adds to the overall effect, but miss out the specification in bar 17 if it creates co-ordination difficulties.

Some useful fingering is supplied on the score. However, alternating hands could be used in the opening bars, with right-hand 2 staying on G and left-hand 2 staying on E, leaving the right-hand thumb to swing down into the Db. Quavers should flow evenly and the finger action may be practised on a table-top, thus focusing attention on the rhythmic flow. Other than where slurs are marked, the touch can be slightly detached – which probably sounds more like the nagging older sibling!

GRADE 2

Lessons will have been learnt from Grade 1, and pupils will probably want to play something similar to their favourite piece from the last exam. The pacing of the preparation, not forgetting the supporting tests, will probably be easier with the experience of Grade 1 safely in the past.

A:1 Bertini *Rondo*

This elegant melody, written by a fine French pianist and pedagogue, needs a young player who can find his or her way around the keyboard with ease. The touch has to be silky smooth, with both hands avoiding bumps in the line and ensuring evenness of tone throughout.

Start by learning with separate hands. The right-hand melody should be smooth and singing (even in a *piano* dynamic), with care taken that the thumb on the C♯ in the first two bars and similar does not fall heavily. The broken arpeggio left-hand accompaniment needs to be gently flowing. Encourage a small circular wrist movement in the left hand (one undulation for each group of three quavers) as well as careful listening, so that any unevenness is identified in the early stages. No doubt this sort of practice will have to be revisited throughout the learning process to ensure smooth execution. Do note the change of articulation in the right hand in bars 10 and 11, where staccato Es give a quirky twist to the melody line.

In addition to conveying the dynamic range from *piano* to *forte*, much should be made of the final crescendo in the last line. This allows a bassoon-like downward arpeggio in the left hand (underneath full orchestral chords in the right) to have the final word.

A:2 Biehl *Allegro grazioso*

This buoyant melody sings merrily over a fairly uncomplicated accompaniment, yet care must be taken over the tempo. If begun too fast, the piece will lose the 'grazioso' feel, which may lead to skidding of the fingers in the later semiquaver passages. The editor's metronome mark is appropriate for finding the light-hearted character.

Some study of the movement's structure may interest your pupil and help in their understanding of basic form. Point out that the music has three sections: in the first section the opening eight bars are repeated almost exactly (bar 15 excepting); in the second section, beginning at bar 16, the right hand's ascending figure is treated to a small variation in bars 20–24. The original melody returns in the final section at bar 24, though bars 28 to the end are another variation, this time of bars 12–16.

The legato and staccato markings need careful observation to make sure that the phrasing detail is shown. Co-ordination could be problematic in bars 21 and 22 with the right hand's semiquavers on weak fingers 3 and 4, but unless a more complicated fingering (passing the thumb) is used, these fingers cannot be avoided. Playing deep into the key here will ensure robust evenness of the fingers. With good rhythmic impetus and technical control, a neat player will find much satisfaction in performing this cheerful Sonatina movement.

A:3 Haydn *Gypsy Dance*

This colourful dance will be fun for the nimble-fingered, though impetuous pupils must beware of hurtling off too quickly and creating a messy blur. Vitality rather than speed is the key to success here. The metronome mark is a safe guide, and a musical student will give the piece a sense of forward direction.

The twisting and turning patterns of the demanding right-hand semiquavers will be troublesome if fingering is not strictly adhered to from the outset. For the dance to get off to a good start, clear articulation in the rising passages of the first two bars (and similar) will be crucial. Maintaining an even tone throughout will require good control of rhythm and careful listening to each note.

The left hand accompanies the right rather like a strumming guitar. A lightness of touch on these crotchet chords will ensure good tonal balance; too much weight on them will obscure the right-hand line. Starting quietly, the first two phrases each make a crescendo to reach a *forte* climax, the change from minor to major adding further emphasis. The second section (bar 9 onwards) is more declamatory in character. Pupils with small hands may need to omit the top notes of the three D minor chords in the left hand of bars 15–16.

Demisemiquavers in the last bar are likely to cause anxiety; these need not be too clearly articulated, however, as they imply a glissando effect – like a small hammer being drawn across the strings of the gypsy's zither.

A:4 Beethoven *Allemande*

The duple metre of the traditional Allemande is here given the unusual twist of being in compound time. Satisfying to play but not for the faint-hearted, this little dance needs good control of double notes and running semiquavers, as well as a buoyant two-in-a-bar.

Special attention should be paid to the articulation. To maintain control at the beginning, the left hand's semiquavers need a deep touch from the first and third fingers. The opening right hand will benefit from staccato on the upbeat chord and on the quaver chords in bars 1 and 2. Take care that the crotchet first beat of bar 1 is held for longer than the quavers. A light staccato touch on the left-hand quavers in bar 3 etc. will point the rhythm.

The section from bars 9 to 16 will require the most work, since the slurring and co-ordination of the notes in bars 9, 10, 13 and 14 is likely to cause difficulties. Experimenting with your student will determine which right-hand fingering best suits the hand. From the upbeat B and G# in bar 8, one suggestion would be 2/1, then in bar 9, for the first four chords, 3/1, 5/3, 4/2, 2/1. A larger hand might manage 2/1 for the first chord of bar 9. The *D.C. al Fine* should be played in the exam.

A:5 J. A. Hiller *Minuetto I*

This sophisticated Minuet is particularly suitable for the more mature student. In six four-bar phrases with the first, second, fifth and sixth phrase using almost the same material, it needs carefully considered dynamics to provide interest. Input could come from your pupil here; this will encourage independent thinking as well as reminding them always to play with dynamic contrast.

The first phrase might be *forte*, the second phrase a little less, and bars 9 and 10 *forte* again with 11 and 12 as an echo. A crescendo would work from bar 13 until the phrase ends in bar 16; this would lead to a *forte* replay of the original theme in bar 17, and the final phrase an echo. Whatever dynamic scheme is chosen, the touch needs to be light. Slurring the first two beats of bar 2 then detaching the third will add elegance, and the left hand needs a detached approach to the crotchets, especially the octave As in bar 24. Legato dotted minims in the left hand in bars 9–15 provide contrast, but to promote flow the first two right-hand chords in bars 9 and 11 should be played with a hint of staccato.

This challenging piece will provide insight into the courtly dance style and serve as good preparation for larger-scale works. Mastering both the key and the organization of the right hand's chords will pay dividends in the future.

A:6 Mozart *Contredance in G*

This vigorous courtly dance with its origin in the English country dance is yet another gem given to us by the prodigious eight-year-old Mozart. Noble in character, it will suit a student with a strong sense of rhythm and nimble fingers.

The pulse must be established firmly from the start, so it is a good idea to encourage your students to count themselves a couple of bars in (but not out loud!). The piece will benefit from pointed accents on the first beats of bars 2 and 4, with a small crescendo in the left hand's repeated Gs in bar 3 leading up to the right-hand arrival on beat 1 of bar 4. Repeated notes at bar 8 (and similarly in bar 16) need a stronger emphasis on the first of the two notes. Bars 11 and 12 might be phrased as an echo of bars 9 and 10. If the fingering of 2/5 on the left hand's chord in bar 13 is tricky, 2/4 may be used instead – however, holding the minim G in the left hand will need lots of separate-hands practice to achieve fluency. The metronome may also be useful in practice, to prevent tearaway pupils from falling over themselves – remember that the dancers are still to be standing at the end with their heads held up high!

B:1 Delibes *Mazurka*

Imagining a performance of this dance from the ballet *Coppélia*, with its energetic steps and leaps, will give a feel for the sheer joy and vitality of this music.

Confidence is needed to negotiate the shifts in right-hand position; sounding the 3rds exactly together is also dependent on careful thought. A few fingerings need particular care: in bar 5 the thumb should be placed over the F♯ in advance, and choice of fingering in bar 6 will need attention. Practising the left-hand accompaniment in block chords, one per bar, will accustom the player to changes in finger shape as the harmonies shift.

Really precise dotted rhythms will convey the dance's spirit and accents at certain points will add strength, provided that the subsidiary beats are lightened. The first note of each repeated figure needs detaching to ensure that the following note sounds clearly. Note that bars 2 and 10 each contain a quaver which should be given full value.

Consider dropping back to *piano* at bar 9 to provide welcome relief from the *forte* elsewhere; a crescendo in the final bars would bring the piece to an exciting, arresting close. Slurring from first to second beat in most bars highlights the one-in-a-bar feel; however, the staccato bass note in bars 5 and 13 gives a momentary shift of musical interest.

B:2 Reinecke *Allegro moderato*

The spirit of Schumann's *Album for the Young* seems never far away in this beautiful piece with its song-like melody and undulating quaver accompaniment. A flowing tempo with few, if any, accents will give direction to the phrases, each of which begins at the half-bar. The numerous, short phrase marks in the right hand should not prevent thinking in two- or four-bar units.

Good legato with no blurring of sounds, especially in scalic figures, is essential to convey this mellifluous style. In contrast, the staccato with slurs (e.g. bars 7 and 11) calls for a slightly detached, lyrical sound. The right hand plays a prominent role throughout, needing firm yet gentle tone, as if sung. Keen listening will ensure that the left hand remains quieter than its partner; keeping the left-hand fingers close to the keys will help to achieve a really subdued sound.

Although *piano* is the only dynamic indicated, gentle rise and fall in tone following the melodic contours will help to sustain musical interest. Bars 4–6, which modulate to A minor, suggest a more dramatic mood, with its dotted rhythms needing careful co-ordination with the left-hand quavers. The pause at bar 8 implies a slight relaxation of pace in the previous bar. The final four bars form a coda during which the mood becomes progressively calmer as the closing chords are reached.

B:3 Reizenstein *The First Snowdrop*

Nothing gives the heart more delight than the sight of the snowdrop, that first spring flower to arrive while the new season awakens. The gently falling phrases and simple textures of this piece seem to represent perfectly this shy yet beautiful flower. The slight air of melancholy suggested by the composer's indication 'Wistfully' can be communicated by mellow tone and graceful phrasing, and at a tempo which is unhurried yet sufficiently flowing to span the long phrases easily.

The opening needs firm yet sweet tone with gently detached repeated notes over a very smooth left hand. Care should be taken here and elsewhere to pace the dotted rhythms accurately against the left hand. The second phrase (beginning at bar 9) conveys a sadder mood by using chromatic notes: at this point, the quaver slurs should be gently shaped with all rests observed. An effective contrast is created if the dynamic is sufficiently quiet as G major is reached at bar 17. The climax occurs at bar 23, at which point tone must be well-matched between the hands in the scale figures. A slight slackening of pace at bar 27 allows the music to ease back to C major. Tone becomes ever quieter towards the end, with care taken to balance the hands effectively.

B:4 Bizet *March from L'arlésienne*

This catchy March, gavotte-like in rhythm with its phrases beginning and ending at the half-bar, has an almost courtly elegance far removed from any military associations. Feeling the natural impetus towards the first beat is essential for the character to emerge, and it might be helpful to think in two, rather than four, beats in a bar to avoid over-stressing less important notes. Care should be taken to keep dotted rhythms really crisp, especially after tied notes, and precise counting will prevent rushing the dotted crotchets in bars 10 and 14.

Some repetition of patterns within the piece will facilitate note learning. In preparation, it might prove beneficial to learn the scale of G minor (a scale now included in the technical requirements for Grade 2). Reliable fingering will ensure accuracy in exam conditions, and practising the left hand alone will develop that all-important confidence over the black keys.

The right-hand phrasing needs clarity, and players should note that the quaver slurring in bar 3 and elsewhere implies a staccato second note. A 'walking bass' effect in the left hand of the first half can be created by detaching the crotchets, slightly emphasizing the first beat. Phrasing is identical between the hands in the second half, and a drop in tone for bars 8–12 provides welcome contrast in an otherwise robust piece.

B:5 Schumann *Trällerliedchen (Humming Song)*

Schumann's *Album for the Young* forms one of the backbones of the piano repertoire and generations of aspiring pianists have enjoyed its many treasures. This beautiful piece, which reflects the composer's lifelong preoccupation with the Lied, will be best approached as a 'song without words'.

Nicht schnell, literally meaning 'not fast', indicates a gently moving, in other words not slow, tempo. Reluctant note-learners will be relieved to discover that the final eight bars are almost identical to bars 1–8, with discrepancies only in bars 22 and 24.

Only through careful listening will your pupil manage a clean legato and good balance of tone between the tune and a quieter accompaniment. No dynamic clues are offered by the composer other than *piano* at the start, but the natural shape of the legato lines can be discovered by singing the melody, breathing at phrase endings. The suggested fingering for the left-hand quavers in the outer sections enables a smooth line to emerge, and thumbs should be kept close to the keys to achieve very subdued repeated offbeat quavers. This applies also to the right hand in bars 9–16 when it combines tune and accompaniment; initial practice of the crotchet melodic line using the suggested fingering before inserting the intervening quavers will help to clarify the texture.

B:6 Robert Washburn *Valse triste*

Sensitive pupils will respond to this soulful waltz with its ambiguous tonality oscillating between F minor and C minor. The pedal is a necessary ingredient for sustaining the harmonies, and the additional challenge of crossing the left hand over the right will doubtless be enjoyed.

A few shifts in the right hand's position need care but otherwise any athleticism is given to the left. Using the pedal in bars 3–4 and elsewhere ensures that the tied bass notes are held through while the left hand moves to the treble register; the pedal should be depressed after the first beat to avoid 'catching' the sounds from the previous bar. The consecutive pedal indications in bars 13–16 imply a change on, not before, the bass C in bar 15.

A tempo of crotchet = 132 allows the music to flow, and a one-in-a-bar feel can be conveyed by keeping the right hand quieter than the left hand's smooth cello-like melody – before the right hand gains more of a solo role for the final few bars. An alternative fingering of 2-1 may be preferred for the left hand of bar 2. The melodic line's characteristic rise and fall contributes to the melancholy mood and, although the dynamic level remains between *mezzo-forte* and *piano*, sensitively shaped phrasing together with a flexible pulse will capture the piece's sadness and longing.

C:1 Eric Clapton *Wonderful Tonight*

What a treat to have this wonderful arrangement of Clapton's classic song in the list! Enjoy the opportunity to research the original, compare versions and decide how to play this particular score, but don't be deceived – its musical and pianistic challenges are as inherent as in any original piece for piano.

A grasp of the melodic idiom is crucial. The grace notes are not Mozart but should be the best the piano can do to imitate a stringbend on the guitar; the timing of these might be varied just a little and they should not be too articulated or apologetic. The dynamic range in the melodic line should also be boldly defined, particularly in the guitar intro (bars 1–4), and the balance clearly focused on the vocal melody of the verse (bars 5–18). This is particularly important in bars 11 onwards where the right hand also has part of the accompaniment.

The harmonic support to the melody is crucial, so the holding of the two harmonic lines must be well rehearsed into the fingers using substitution where necessary (e.g. bar 5). The left hand should also provide good rhythmic support under the more flexible melody.

Keep the tempo relaxed, and, while this should not happen in the exam, your pupil might occasionally try an improvisation Clapton-style – this can only help with the overall feel and mood.

C:2 Elissa Milne *Mozzie*

This is another fresh-faced gem which will be deservedly popular but is not as easy as it sounds or looks. The co-ordination between the hands in bars 5–7 will catch many out, and the final two bars are easy to misjudge.

Bars 5–7 will need very slow, methodical practice; encourage short, light 3rds in the right hand with a more positive tone in the left and a deliberate lift for the rests and the ends of phrases. The right hand's jump over bars 15–16 will need to become well established in the physical memory, and the chords in bar 16 should have a strong bounce from the wrist.

The 'Persistently' marking conveys the importance of a firm rhythmic identity achieved by a rock-steady pulse and carefully executed articulation. If the piece is performed as written – with good rounded fingers and a bright yet not heavy tone, observing all the dynamic markings – it will sound convincing. Some subtleties, though, will help the personality. The grace note in bar 4 should be cheekily squashed into the A with perhaps a decrescendo through the quavers so that the final staccato is not too pointed. The hairpin in bar 9 can be playfully exaggerated and the penultimate bar's *fortissimo* played with strong and rhythmic fingers to set up the surprise of the final soft-pawed D.

C:3 Giles Swayne *Whistling Tune*

How often have we seen people walking along the street whistling a tune that few of us recognize? A first hearing of this unusual yet endearing piece may not immediately entice the performer, but it is worth persevering; the image of this happy whistler with few worldly cares is vivid and the piece will easily become a popular choice if presented with a little imagination.

The melody needs to be simply played, not with any musical exaggeration, but with a gently dynamic shape and a relaxed manner. Avoid, therefore, too literal an interpretation of the staccato on the last note of each phrase; it should match the staccato of the left hand which isn't very short – just a light footstep. Consistent and organized fingering in the left hand will help it remember where to go and avoid hesitation.

The middle section is a little more robust. The staccato could be shorter here, perhaps reflecting some frustration as the sun goes behind a cloud. A few legato and unhurried bars to calm the mind come before the pause (the moment of waiting for the sun to reappear before continuing the happy stroll?). All of this imagery can be conveyed in the tone, dynamics and articulation. It is important to challenge the imagination throughout, conjuring up the image of the whistler disappearing around a distant corner at the final, delicate decrescendo.

C:4 Bart *Reviewing the Situation*

The cheek and deviousness of Fagin's song from *Oliver!* is marvellously translated in this wonderful arrangement. A knowledge of the original words and of Fagin's character is a must, as the performance demands some playfulness with the pulse, a subtlety of melodic shape and a slightly detached left hand underneath a vocal, legato melody.

The tempo (crotchet = *c*.116) is perhaps a little fast, and to communicate the humour effectively the piece should not be metronomically rigid – as the pauses on the first two notes infer. Easing in the tempo through the first full bar works well. Bars 16 to 28 need imagination, an awareness of the song-like character, perhaps with slight breaths between phrases and just a little increased momentum before the rallentando.

The left hand shouldn't be spiky but lightly detached, similar to a pizzicato, and with a light, still hand so that the right-hand melody can sing through. Dynamic shading of the melody with a slight decrescendo at the ends of phrases can then be achieved without affecting the balance.

Finally, so many pieces with a flourish at the end finish in a tangle. 'Very fast!' does not mean faster than can be played comfortably, and these bars need conscientious work so that the fingers don't let the performer down on the day. The final triumphant chord is then fully justified!

C:5 Hurd *Fanfare from Bagatelles*

One of the puzzles in this haunting piece is its title. The arpeggiated figures are like a fanfare but not as redolent of brass as the title would suggest – more a ghostly re-enactment perhaps. However, with conflicting harmonies and the stirring ending wonderfully juxtaposed, this piece is a captivating choice.

Pedal, while not essential, conveys the atmosphere and should be achievable by some pupils. Initially change only at the beginning of each bar but in bars 9 and 10 change mid-bar, and hold as instructed in bars 11 and 12.

The perfect tempo suggestion of dotted crotchet = 56 gives time to shape the phrases dynamically as marked. The fingering is not so predictable; consider an arpeggio-based fingering in the opening, and in bars 7 and 8 the left hand could use 3-2-1 up to the B in bar 8 followed by 2-3-5 for the arpeggio figure starting on A♭. There are two solutions to bar 13: one is for the right hand to reach the A by crossing the third finger over the fifth (on F); the other is to swap the hands around, the right hand replaying the F while the left reaches up to the A.

The 'Fanfare' of the title is there at the end; confident and bright quavers are needed here with a bold *stringendo*, using the *rit.* to delay the final F octave and convey a cheeky end.

C:6 Manfred Schmitz *Tango für Elise*

Those of you who have endlessly heard pupils playing the first bars of Beethoven's *Für Elise* will immediately get the joke of the opening. Elise of course would never have known the Tango, as its origins are much later, and Beethoven undoubtedly would have been less than inclined to dance it even if she had!

An understanding of the Tango is a prerequisite to learning this piece, as the nuance in the left hand's Latin rhythm should be conveyed. Correctly done, this should prevent a misinterpretation of the slurred chords across bars 2–3, the second of which should be played again, with a light staccato touch after a longer, slightly emphasized chord on the fourth beat of the previous bar.

Taking the expressive markings literally and avoiding an accented first note in the right hand's phrases will help the character. Lightly detaching the final notes of some phrases will point the syncopation that follows and suggest the slight emphasis on the accents; anything too aggressive will spoil the charm.

A solid and reliable beat in the staccato crotchet chords in the left hand will set up the rhythmic fun and games elsewhere, and exploring a range of dynamics beyond those actually written will help the dancers in their slightly arrogant dance.

GRADE 3

Perhaps it is time to be a little more adventurous in the choice of pieces, now that exams are quite a familiar experience. Something of quite a different style might broaden the pupil's outlook, so do explore the alternative pieces as well as the printed selection.

A:1 Anon. *Menuet in G*

This well-known, delightful Minuet will be popular among the younger pianists for its charm and pretty melody. With its arpeggio figures it falls nicely under the fingers but there are some tricky corners. It is only too common to hear unusual rhythmic interpretations of bars 15 and 39, and hesitation at the jumps at the beginning of bars 19, 29 and so on.

Some clapping and aural work should easily sort the triplet rhythm – it is crucial that your student establishes a rhythmic template before going away to learn the notes. The jumps will be helped by thinking ahead, but also by plenty of shadow jumping. It is a good idea to play bar 18 but delay the final note in each hand until the performer knows exactly where the hand is travelling to. One approach to encourage a quick movement might be to play the final note of bar 18 as a quaver and arrive at the beginning of the next a quaver early.

Once comfortable and fluent, the piece should have an innate sense of the dance. Light second and third beats in bars 2, 4–6 and so on will help the charm, as will an arch-shaped use of dynamic through the two-bar phrases. Don't take the editorial couplet phrasing at the end of bars 5, 6 etc. too literally as this will encourage an undesirable hiccup; instead, think of the couplet as leading into the first beat of the next bar.

Dynamically the piece calls out for variety and interest. The minor middle section needs to be enough of a contrast, the brighter sounds saved for the beginning and end – with perhaps a ritardando in the final bar.

A:2 T. Morley *Now is the month of maying*

This superb arrangement of a well-known Madrigal is a piece to conjure up the beginning of summer in the cold winter months. A lively performance should immediately bring to mind the sprightly words, so it is worth having a quick look at the text; an awareness of the generally monosyllabic words will help to convey just the right spirit and energy. It is also an excellent piece to stimulate discussion of modal melodies and harmonies.

In the opening and similar bars the touch needs to be a crisp, bright yet lightly detached, achieved with energy in the fingertips close to the keys and yet avoiding a heavy left hand. Also essential is leaning into the minims in bars 2, 4 and so on. A little give in the wrist here will allow a warm sound and encourage the hand to stay in the key just a little longer, giving a feminine ending to the phrase.

To add interest it will be important to colour the piece with a variety of articulation. One idea would be to contrast the legato lines (e.g. bars 9 and 18–19) with a more detached style. While most of the performance should have a decisive sense of pulse and rhythm, a little more rhythmic pliancy (but still with clearly defined articulation) can lend personality to the more lyrical phrases.

The suggested dynamic markings are an excellent starting point but as they are not Morley's originals you can enjoy exploring alternatives. Bear in mind that within a limited two-part texture it must not become too heavy-footed in tone, and the player's ears will be the best judge of this. Overall there should be no hint of struggle – instead, technical ease and polish will give the performance life and vitality right through to the final 'fa la la la la'.

A:3 attrib. Mozart *Andante in C*

This is a Mozart aria by any other name, or perhaps a duet, and it has a delightful melody and much charm and poise. The notes may not look difficult but the complexity lies in the control, musical nuance and balance. With this in mind, consistent and organized fingering will be crucial in educating just the right sound into each finger.

In the opening both 'singers' need to be as legato as possible, so within the phrase lines at least one note in the right hand should join without a break to the next: the C to the E in the first group of 3rds and the G to the C between the second and third chords; similarly in bar 2, the top notes of the 6ths. For a little colour, the fourth beat in bars 1–2 might be lightly lifted to throw a little nuance onto the first beat of the next, though always within a dynamically shaped phrase; also take care to shade the repeated 3rds in bar 3 to lead to a feminine ending in bar 4.

Details like these will reward the musical student, though an intrusive left hand will soon spoil these admirable intentions, particularly in the middle section. The quavers should be extremely light, fingers close to the key and not too articulated while the melody sings eloquently above. Just a little more tone in the bottom notes of the quavers from the end of bar 10 will provide a warm counter-melody.

A good tempo should allow control and give breadth to the piece, although this may make the player feel rather exposed during the rests at the end. However the rests should be enjoyed, not just counted, allowing time for a contented sigh before the final (orchestral) chords.

A:4 Attwood *Allegro assai*

This joyous movement requires two things technically: a comfortable physical freedom in the right hand and a fluent ease in the Alberti bass of the left. It will not present difficulties for those pupils who have mastered the scale of F major; the challenge is in bringing these scalic figures to life with expressive articulation and musical shape.

Initial work should concern the opening left-hand figures. Some pupils will have no problem in negotiating them, but as many an examiner will tell you, such pupils are in a minority! The Alberti figures can be uneven at best, and at worst they can slow the pulse down considerably. The secret lies in avoiding a tight, tense hand – something that readily creeps in if the hand is held still above the keys and the fingers are over-drilled, which can lead to excessive tension and an invasive sound. It is better to relax into the bottom notes, possibly holding them a little longer to provide harmonic support, and keeping the finger movement above to a minimum.

In the places where the left hand jumps there may be some hesitation. To iron this out, use the rests to the full. In practising bars 13–14, for instance, stopping on the second beat of bar 13 and ensuring that the left hand has already travelled to its next note will pay huge dividends.

The right hand is guided across the keys by its melody. Releasing weight behind the fingers when the hand ascends will enable a smooth crescendo; a dance-like choreography of the fingers and hand will help the phrasing and character elsewhere. Explore the dynamics to the full without outgrowing the two-part texture tonally; aim to keep the listener fully absorbed and captivated.

A:5 Clementi *Vivace*

If the F major scales and Alberti bass of the Attwood are technically too much for your pupil, the C major scales in this jolly sonatina movement with its easier left-hand figurations may prove more comfortable. Although not a difficult movement technically, and predictable in its patterns, it needs much more musical detail as a result. The essence of the piece will only be conveyed if there is a subtle use of balance and the melody given charisma and nuance throughout. The *Vivace* marking should not therefore be taken too literally, and the suggested dotted crotchet = 63 works well.

Depending on the edition there may be a multitude of markings over the broken chords of the left hand. Ignore these! Your pupil should instead concentrate on playing them smoothly and lightly, with a gradual decrescendo through the bar as the figure rises to avoid it interfering and sounding too 'notey'. The repeated chords should also be light regardless of the dynamic, allowing the right hand to remain at the fore.

A characterful performance will rely on the articulation, dynamic shape and phrasing of the melody. Essential to conveying the naive cheek and humour of the piece, the performer must develop a natural physical freedom at the keyboard, a lightness of the second and third beats (particularly through repeated notes), and an eloquence of dynamic shading through the runs. Avoid a 'bump' at the beginning of these runs, which often start on the upbeat. Explore with your pupil far beyond the given dynamic suggestions, which should be taken as a starting point only.

A placing of the final chord, with a small *rit.* just before it, will help establish the end of the fun and games.

A:6 Weber *Scherzo*

This is a refreshingly different piece and a welcome new addition to the syllabus. Essentially in C major, the Scherzo begins with a joke in the relative minor and the Trio is predominantly in F major to tease the audience; this is coupled with more than a hint of an invitation to a dance.

There are downsides to Weber's inventiveness, however, as the piece presents some technical difficulties in its left-hand jumps and in the chordal right hand of the Trio. Particular attention needs to be paid over bars 12–13 where the left hand jumps at speed; plenty of shadow jumping will be required, stopping on the bar's first beat to check that the left hand has correctly measured its jump and then on to the second beat to make sure the hand has covered the chord. Make use of the quaver rest in bar 16 to get hands quickly in position for starting the Trio.

For the Trio's right-hand chords to be as legato as possible without pedal the hand will need to stay on the keys until just before the bar-line, when it moves gently to the next chord. This will give each chord due weight and shape the line dynamically to the top C.

Overly strident left-hand chords in the opening will destroy the humour. Just a little more activity in the fingers on the first chord of each bar and lighter second and third beats will give the Scherzo more rhythmic impetus. All right-hand melodic scalic passages must be musically shaped, observing the phrasing to create fluidity.

When repeating the Scherzo after the da capo, add just a little nuance to the top Gs to help the dance along.

B:1 Absil *Petit berger (Little Shepherd)*

The picture of a shepherd boy playing his flute to calm the sheep at nightfall is a familiar Romantic image. This rather plaintive melody, set against slow-moving chords, conjures up the loneliness of a hillside vigil.

The left hand must move as smoothly as possible. The fingering for the first four bars (1/5-2/3) involves the second finger reaching across the thumb to the F♯, so allow the wrist to rise and fall gently from chord to chord. The second four-bar group, using 2/5-1/3, involves less movement. If preferred, this second fingering can be used throughout the piece: where it replaces the first fingering, move the hand forward into the keys so that the thumb is already in position for the F♯ (e.g. bar 1). It would also be necessary to play the F♯ in bar 8 with the thumb in anticipation.

The phrasing is interesting. The legato lines indicate that the melody does not fall into the usual four-bar phrases, but into a long, seamless eight-bar phrase followed by one of five bars. Thereafter it becomes more fragmented until the music fades into silence. Be sure to count carefully through the last two bars, listening closely to the dying sounds. The dynamics provide clear guidance, and the suggested metronome mark of dotted crotchet = *c*.50 allows the player time to be expressive.

While the left hand provides a quiet background, the melody must be played with a clearly projected singing tone. It would be helpful to hear it played on a flute – if a flautist can be found, this piece would make a lovely duet.

Technically this is not a difficult piece, and will appeal to the imaginative pupil who enjoys colour and mood.

B:2 Loeschhorn *Study in F*

Sometimes a study has little in it to attract pupils, but give it a title (this might be called 'Spring Song') or ask your pupils to think of their own, and this charming melody, with its touches of colourful harmony, will appeal to many.

The phrasing is typically Classical, starting with a 2 + 2 + 4 bar structure. At bar 6 (also bars 10 and 14) the composer indicates that the melody should flow seamlessly into the next bar. The last eight bars form a coda, repeating the perfect cadence chords no fewer than four times. However, highlights of the harmony are heard in bars 5–6 where it hints at the key of G minor, and at bars 9–12 where it passes through F minor, with the added spice of an augmented 6th chord on the last beat of bar 11. These special features should be explained to pupils to help them bring more expression to their playing; an ideal way to become aware of the harmony (and speed up the learning process) is to practise the left hand in block chords first.

Pedal may be used in a few carefully selected places. For instance, in bars 1 and 5, pedal from first beat to third, and in bar 6 from third beat to the first of the next bar (and similar). Adding pedal to the minims in the last four bars will make it easier to join the cadence chords smoothly. So-called 'finger-pedalling' is required in bars 7, 15, 17 and 19 so that the left hand's semibreve C can be held through the bar.

A metronome mark of crotchet = *c*.104 (up to 108) will allow the music to unfold in a carefree, relaxed manner.

B:3 Saint-Saëns *L'éléphant (The Elephant)*

This piece from *The Carnival of the Animals* may already be familiar to your pupils, but it will be even better if they can hear just how ponderous it sounds on the double bass.

Balance will be an important issue. While this animal is undoubtedly heavy, it would be unmusical to play the right-hand chords as loudly as the melody, except perhaps at the main cadence points in bars 19–20 and at the end. The choice of tempo is also crucial. The suggested metronome mark of crotchet = *c*.112 offers good momentum while allowing for the composer's elephant-inspired humour!

Slurs and staccato marks should be carefully observed, although for this piece the staccato should not be too short. Although not essential, touches of pedal may be employed to add sonority to the opening dotted minims and to mark the slurred notes in bars 5, 7 and 8 (and similar). However, the pedal must be released in time for the rests (bars 2 and 4) and the staccato notes (bar 5 etc.).

To imitate the bowing of the double bass, it would not be wrong to play unslurred crotchets (like those in bars 9–11) in a slightly detached manner, and in bar 19 the *fortissimo* chords should be clearly separated. Your pupil will enjoy the extrovert dropping of the arms into these chords.

For the *mezzo-forte* passage at bar 21, bring down the volume of the right-hand notes to at least *mezzo-piano* so that the last *forte* phrase ends the performance with a flourish.

B:4 Gounod *Les pifferari (The Bagpipers)*

The scene could be a busy market at Christmas: last-minute shopping, excited children, and the joyous sound of music filling the air. Bagpipers have come to town!

With only four chords to learn in the left hand, this would seem to be an easy option, but the constant repetition can lead to confusion. Start by practising just the lower notes, focusing on the movement of the fingers: 5-3 (upward step), then 2-4 (downward). Later, when adding the thumb notes, keep the attention firmly on those moving fingers, allowing only a little space between the accented chords so that they provide a sturdy background.

The melody will need a lively attack. It is in regular eight-bar phrases, beginning with an upbeat group. In figures with rests (i.e. bar 6), staccato is effective, but longer groups of quavers (e.g. bars 14 and 22) could be more legato to create contrast and ease of performance. If the crotchet-quaver figures are also to be detached, give the crotchets more length than the quavers.

It is clear that dynamics will be important. Although *forte* is indicated for more than two-thirds of the piece, it should be remembered that persistently loud tone becomes tiring on the ear. A little less volume would sound convincing at bar 21 (second beat); then with a crescendo from bar 30 it builds to a climax marking the start of the last section at bar 37 (second beat). Care will be needed to control the long diminuendo towards the end, and *una corda* pedal will help the last six bars. The dance fades into the distance as the listener makes their way home.

33

B:5 Reinecke *Andantino*

A mood of regret and tenderness pervades this attractive piece. It will appeal to many but especially to those who like to express their feelings through their playing.

The suggested metronome marks – dotted crotchet = 76 for the opening *Andantino* and quaver = 126 for the middle section (described as *Etwas langsamer* – 'somewhat slower') – are confusing and prove to be rather extreme. It would be better to have dotted-crotchet speeds for both sections: somewhere around 60–66 for the *Andantino* and 40–42 for the middle section would be more suitable for the character of the music.

Both left hand and right take turns in playing melody and accompaniment in the outer sections, so this will make a useful study in balance and tone production. It would be helpful to play the melody alone at first, so that it is heard as one long line moving from hand to hand. The accompaniment is to be played with a tenuto staccato touch, so encourage your pupil to keep the fingers in contact with the keys and play the repeated chords as smoothly as possible.

In the middle section the left hand takes the accompanying role throughout, although at bars 13–16, and a few bars later, there is an important canonic feature to highlight. Co-ordination could be a challenge in bar 13 (and similar), so make a point of stressing the right hand's dotted-quaver chord so that it is not disturbed by the left-hand quavers. A tiny ritenuto towards the pause in bar 22 and a 'breath' at the double bar-line makes a musical point before returning to the first theme and original tempo.

B:6 Sandré *Go to Sleep*

Cradle songs have universal appeal, loved by young and old, and this attractive example makes a good choice for the more sensitive pupil.

Notice first the sustained 'pedal' notes in the left hand. In the first section, the G is held throughout each bar, only to be replayed in bar 8 to complete the phrase. It will demand skilful finger independence, so check and listen carefully for clarity, keeping the hand as relaxed as possible. The melody should be shaped according to the phrase marks. Inventing words can help with inflections and create character – and making up your own can be fun. For instance, 'Sleep now, my little one, sleep. Mother sings you a gentle lullaby' traces the outline of the first two phrases.

Grace notes are an important feature, adding a pleasing lilt, but must be delicate so as not to disturb the mood. In bar 6 (and similar) where two grace notes appear together, they should be played on the beat as shown. Elsewhere, it is a matter of choice. Dynamics never rise above *piano*, and *con sord(ini)* indicates the use of the *una corda* pedal.

In the middle section (bars 9–16) the semiquavers are merely decorative, so keep them light and feel them flowing towards the longer notes. At this point, melodic interest shifts to the left hand, so the balance must be adjusted accordingly. The little lines under right-hand chords in bar 11 (and similar) are just tenuto marks, not accents, and at bar 16, ease the tempo only slightly at the *rit.*; save the more significant slowing down for the final three bars. Like Schumann's wonderful portrayal in 'Child Falling Asleep' from his *Scenes from Childhood*, this piece catches those mysterious moments when we drift away into sleep.

C:1 Chow Shu San *Tell You*

This beautiful and atmospheric Chinese piece, suited to the more thoughtful player, evokes sounds and images of ancient instruments such as the stringed erhu, and the bamboo flute. For your students to understand the meditative sound-world for this piece, encourage them to listen to recordings of Chinese orchestras and singers.

'Rubato' (or robbed time) can be a difficult concept, but naturally artistic pupils will have no trouble with the space and freedom that the phrasing requires. This is a piece which needs demonstration from the teacher to inspire and to show just how much elasticity the timing can afford.

The first four bars are a contemplative introduction before the left hand begins to sing the wise and telling melody at the end of bar 5. The *mezzo-forte* marking here applies to the left hand; encourage delicacy in the right-hand decorations (bar 6 etc.) so that the left hand's melody is not covered.

The composer marks *con Ped.* at the beginning; in general, legato pedalling works throughout. Occasional blurring of sounds – for example, when holding the pedal through the first two beats of bars 6 and 7 and similar – will give the right atmosphere, but if pedalling in that way it is even more important that the right hand is light and quiet, otherwise the texture will become too muddled.

The last line needs careful organization of rhythm. Also note that the arpeggio marking for the final right-hand chord points downwards, requiring the notes of the chord to be played from E down to A. Hold the last chord for its full value plus a pause, so as not to disturb the peaceful atmosphere too early.

C:2 Hanna, Barbera and Curtin *Top Cat!*

Familiarity with the star character and theme tune of this vintage American cartoon series will make this delightful piece a hit of the grade, though it is by no means an easy option. Experience tells us, though, that if a student is fascinated by a well-known catchy tune, results are quickly and eagerly achieved (often a revelation to teacher and pupil alike!).

The 'Bright swing tempo' suggests that this jaunty piece will be most successful with swung quavers (i.e., that the first quaver of a pair is roughly twice the length of the second) – with the exception of bars 6 and 8 which remain straight. There are, however, other factors that can make a piece of music swing, including: a natural ease of delivery and facility at the keyboard; a solid beat to underpin the music; and an ability to feel the syncopation (especially in offbeat accents such as those on the second quaver of the second beat of bars 15, 16, 24 and 26).

A confident approach to the opening right-hand chords (with an accent on the first) sets the scene. To complement, the prowling bass-line in the left hand is played with a dabbing, *mezzo* staccato touch (indicated by both a staccato and a tenuto mark on the same note). Lighter notes are indicated later by staccato marks alone, such as those in bars 6, 8, 23 and 24. Those with small hands may need to omit top notes of the left hand's octave Gs in bars 17 and 18, along with the final octave of the piece to play only the outer Cs in each hand.

This piece has the potential to win your student popularity and kudos among friends when played at school concerts, guaranteeing that he or she is 'the leader of the gang' in true Top Cat fashion.

C:3 Hold *Quajira*

One can immediately feel the infectious and bouncy Latin beat of this music, which should be easy to pick up once the dual time-signature is understood. In fact, the rhythm is probably the best place to start: take turns with your student, with one of you clapping three crotchets and the other six quavers, and then gradually let your student take over clapping the sequence of both patterns. Once this is established go to the note-learning and get the pattern of the left hand's first two bars under control before adding the right hand.

The various accents and articulation markings here have different roles. The pointed accents over the first three notes in the left hand and later in the right (e.g. bar 5) are played staccato with a short, sharp attack. The tenuto marks over the first and fourth quavers in bar 2 etc. stress the rhythm, and require a more weighty emphasis – though the quavers must also be staccato as marked.

The piece needs good dynamic colouring. You might add an extra crescendo from bar 11, reaching a *forte* at bar 15, and this will brighten the sound of the passage as it modulates through E minor to G major. The flow is interrupted by pauses at the end of bars 27 and 30. This gives a feeling of suspense and asks two questions, which are then answered in the return to the home key of C major from bar 31, and in the strong ending of the accented final note.

This piece will be a winner with candidates who have a strong sense of rhythm and who enjoy being flamboyant in performance.

C:4 Mike Cornick *Waltz in F*

This smooth jazz waltz is likely to be a hit with everyone; it will especially appeal to musicians who enjoy a more laid-back style of piano playing and delicious jazz harmonies. The composer gives instructions about how to swing the quavers, and this applies only to single quavers (bars 2, 7, 9, 11, 14 and 17), which need to be neatly tucked in, nonchalantly, before the bar's third beat. An overall feeling of one-in-a-bar will ensure that the waltz really dances.

To establish the legato indicated at the beginning of the piece, spend time practising separate hands first. This will ensure that the left hand sings out the sustained dotted-minim bass notes with a slightly stronger voice compared to the chords in the upper part of the hand. The exception to this is in bars 13–16, where the top notes of the chords (G to F♯ and F♮ to E) emerge as a counter-melody to the right hand to colour the sumptuous harmony.

Judicious use of pedalling is implied by the marking *con Ped.* Legato pedalling (i.e. down with the second beat of the left hand and lifting again on the first beat of the next bar) will work for the most part except, again, in bars 13–16; it may be easier to omit the pedal in bars 14 and 16 to give clarity to the texture.

Enjoy the cool ending! When the harmony changes to a D♭ 7th chord in bar 20 before resolving on the tonic F, followed by the final note in the bass, you can't help but want to whisper a jazz 'yeah'. . .

C:5 Richard Kershaw *Jack's Asleep!*

This very clever jazz variation on the round *Frère Jacques* cannot fail to appeal to all ages. A bouncy but steady tempo is encouraged by adopting a slightly faster metronome mark of crotchet = 100. The choice whether or not to swing the syncopated rhythm is entirely up to the player; examiners will accept either if the composer has not expressed a preference. Whichever is decided, the dynamic is a bold *mezzo-forte* to start with, and you might consider working up to *forte* at bar 9 to brighten the sound at this higher register. The diminuendo requested from bar 13 should not begin too quietly as the dynamic needs to reduce all the way through to the end of the piece, where *pianississimo* is called for.

Although by no means essential for an effective performance, the addition of some pedal would enhance the style of the piece. If your pupil has experience of legato pedalling, you could introduce it over bars 8–9 to join the left-hand chords and again in bar 11 through to the end of bar 16. The 'bells' heard in bars 13–16 are those of a more distant kind; take care that your pupil's enthusiasm to play these groovy harmonies does not cause forced sound here.

Unlike the rhyme, which leaves unanswered the question 'are you sleeping?', here the composer adds four bars (17 to the end) which tell the player to get slower, suggesting that Jacques does fall asleep. In the final two bars one can imagine his mother descending the stairs slowly, with a finger over her lips whispering, 'Sleep well, my little one' (*Dormez bien, mon petit*).

C:6 Pēteris Plakidis *Quiet Walk in the Forest*

Here we have the welcome opportunity to study music of our time. This excellent example of a descriptive piece from the *Spectrum 4* collection demands good counting (the metre changes often) and an ability to move around the keyboard freely, yet sensitively. A sinister left hand (which the composer says 'should sound like humming') creeps around in the undergrowth, while the right hand provides the atmospheric bird-calls heard high up and the noises of the scurrying animals of the forest.

Without a doubt the counting will try your student's patience, with the transition of bars 3–4, 6–7, and the final bar 17 being the most troublesome spots. In bars 4 and 7 the left hand comes in quicker than expected with the first beat, with the right hand having had only a quaver rest to negotiate a big leap. In the final bar the placing of the semiquaver chord in the right hand will cause difficulty; the best way to do this is to count quavers from the low C on beat 4 of bar 16 through to the end. The tied left-hand C should be held for a further two beats after the right hand's last chord to let the sound die away.

Although written with the key signature of four flats, the tonality is uncertain throughout; it finally settles down on C, maintaining a mysterious air to the end. This piece will help to calm your pupils and encourage them to listen to themselves more. The dynamics do not go above *mezzo-piano*, and perhaps the most significant word in the title is the word 'Quiet'!

GRADE 4

Many of the List B pieces will benefit from some pedal, but if your pupil's legs are too short there is always an alternative piece from the extensive lists. The musical character of candidates often becomes more firmly established at this stage and they can play to their strengths, making sure the pieces are contrasted in tempo and mood.

A:1 G. Benda *Allegro assai*

The Allegro movements written by this Czech composer often seem to exude good humour, and this one is no exception. It would also be a good choice for players with a limited stretch, as it all lies neatly under the hands.

The term *Allegro assai* is often thought of as 'very fast', but *assai* has several meanings including 'enough' which is more appropriate for this piece. A tempo of crotchet = *c*.84 (up to crotchet = 92) will allow the amiable nature of the music to emerge.

The small lines on the quaver noteheads (see first few bars) are tenuto marks, not accents, so they should be held a little rather than played staccato, and the similarly marked crotchets (bars 5 and 6 etc.) should be just slightly detached. Other articulation marks – staccato and slurs – are clearly shown and, together with the dynamics, will provide ample scope for expression. With so much detail in the score, pedal is best avoided.

At bar 9 (and similar) the new phrase is marked *forte* but overlaps the end of the previous phrase, so the left-hand crotchet should be quieter than the right hand's melody notes. The two passages with repeated offbeat quavers (at bars 33 and 37) must be handled sensitively. Begin quietly and build the crescendo gradually so that *forte* is held back until the first of the semiquavers. The appoggiaturas in bar 13 (and similar) take half the value of the quaver so that the groups all sound like four semiquavers.

This delightful piece presents few technical problems for the performer and will be fun to play.

A:2 Handel *Allegro in F*

The sheer exuberance of this Allegro will ensure its popularity with pianists of all ages. It has the characteristics of an Italian corrente, and the suggested tempo of crotchet = *c*.104 will allow for sparkle without danger.

It will sound stylish to detach many of the crotchets, and to play most of the quavers staccato. Slurs are indicated on some first-beat quavers, helping to emphasize without accenting, but others may also be slurred. For instance, at the approach to the main cadences (bars 7, 15 and 25), an additional slur on the second pair of quavers, or even second and third pairs, will strengthen the sense of closure.

It is essential that semiquavers flow comfortably; a useful practice strategy would be to take out all the scale figures and practise them individually. Start with bar 1, playing from first beat to third, and answer that with the left hand's rising scale (bar 4), matching the speed and evenness of flow. Pupils will quickly realize that these patterns are familiar, and even at the earliest stages they can be played quite quickly. It would also be worthwhile giving extra attention to bars 10–11 (and 12–13) where the scale figures must flow on uninterrupted by the placing of the left-hand chord. Some players may find it difficult to stretch the chord in bar 11, even if they lower the wrist so that fingers 1 and 5 are on the very edge of the keys. If so, the best solution would be to omit the G – at least it would match what follows in bar 13.

The suggested dynamic marks will provide plenty of colour, and a ritenuto in the penultimate bar will bring this exciting piece to a strong conclusion.

A:3 J. S. Bach *Bourrée 1*

Of the various character dances found in the Baroque suite, the Bourrée is among the liveliest. Despite its minor mode, this dance is cheerful in character and should be felt as two-in-a-bar. The metronome mark of minim = *c*.88 works well.

Before commencing serious practice, it would be advisable to discuss the fingering with each pupil, as hand shape and size can affect the final decision. The fingering found in many editions may not suit everyone, so encourage pupils to contribute their own ideas. Deciding to play most of the crotchets in a detached manner (particularly in the left hand) is not only stylish, but will immediately free the hand so that it can jump into position rather than using fingering that always connects from note to note. For instance, in bar 4 it may feel more comfortable for the left hand to jump to the first note (F♯) with the second finger.

In the right-hand melody, a few of the first-beat crotchets will sound effective if they are sustained and joined to the following quavers. These

41

occur in bars 7, 11, 15 and 17. The usual practice methods of separate hands and then hands-together, slowly, should build up a safe technique. Later, practising in different rhythms can be helpful.

As this is a quick dance, little ornamentation is needed, but it would be attractive, and not difficult, to add mordents (lower) to the last right-hand note of each section. Because of the quick tempo, the mordent in bar 6 could be reduced to a simple acciaccatura D.

The suggested dynamic marks are helpful, and if followed will ensure that the performance is shapely and colourful.

A:4 J. C. F. Bach *Angloise in D*

Angloise or Anglaise was the name given to a piece written in the style of an English country dance. This one is like a hornpipe and needs bright tone and crisp articulation.

The recommended ABRSM publication suggests that left-hand quavers should be played staccato, so where notes have wedge-shaped articulation marks (see bar 3) it would be appropriate to give them a little more emphasis. In bars 10 and 11, where the wedges are over crotchets, avoid making the notes too short. Imagine the dancers are clapping their hands to add excitement. It is also stylish to detach the upbeat quavers at beginnings of phrases. This gives a spring to the step and places the accent effortlessly on to the first beat of the bar.

If the ornament over the cadence in bar 12 proves a stumbling-block, try this easier solution. First practise just the three pairs of notes with fingers 4/2, 3/1 and 2/1, as though they are equal quaver beats. Try to keep them as smooth as possible, and allow the hand to float off with the last pair to shape the end of the phrase. Then simply add a triplet semiquaver group (G-A-G) with the E of the second chord.

The Trio section moves to the subdominant key of G, and the editor's suggestion of a slightly slower tempo and quieter dynamics conjures up the image of a solo dancer taking centre stage to display some intricate steps. The accompaniment becomes more static and legato, adding emphasis to this change of mood. Then with the *D.C. al Fine* the pace quickens again, and everyone joins in to bring the dance to a spirited conclusion.

A:5 Beethoven *4th movt from Symphony No. 1*

It is fun for the pianist to dip into the orchestral repertoire occasionally. This cheery extract offers a wonderful opportunity to develop different types of staccato, while enjoying the exuberance of the music.

Beethoven marks this movement *Allegro molto e vivace*, so nimble fingers will be required. The opening scale needs to run crisply and easily, and at first your pupil could practise it on the surface of the keys only. Fingers should tap audibly on each key, allowing just the last note to sound as the fifth finger springs upwards. In this way it can be played quite fast, encouraging the realization that all the notes are contained within just one arm movement. When playing normally, begin lightly and build the crescendo from the fourth note (C) towards the first beat of bar 2.

The different types of staccato can be clearly identified in the right hand of bars 17–23. Starting *piano*, the quavers in bars 17 and 19 will be finger staccato, while the repeated 3rds at bars 20–21 will be hand (or wrist) staccato. Begin this group close to the keys, increasing the movement with the crescendo. At bar 22 the staccato will become a full arm stroke. Similar patterns of notes should be treated the same way, so sometimes co-ordination will be a problem. Separate-hands practice will be helpful.

If the edition you are using shows the hands colliding on B in bar 29, it would be better to play this note with the right hand to keep the melody intact.

Beethoven's own metronome mark for this movement was hair-raisingly fast (minim = 80), but here the suggested crotchet = 126 is both realistic and quick enough to convey the vitality and good humour of the music.

A:6 Mozart *Rondo in D*

The little keyboard pieces by the child Mozart provide a wealth of delightful material for the aspiring pianist. Written in 1765 while Mozart was in London, this Rondo is light-hearted and graceful, dance-like in character.

It is best felt as two beats in a bar, as befits its metronome mark of dotted crotchet = 60. Articulation and dynamic marks have also been provided, and serve as a useful guide. However, it would not be incorrect to omit the slur across the bar-line into bar 3, and to play both quaver chords staccato in bar 7, thus offering a simpler execution. The left-hand Alberti figures will need special attention to achieve agility and buoyancy. Encourage your pupil to keep the arm light and well supported, with fingers active but close to the keys. Look out for the sudden change of pattern in bars 3 and 7; it would be easy to miss it.

There is a change of mood in the middle section when it shifts to the tonic minor and its relative major of F (a key quite remote from D major). Playing in a more legato style will help to highlight these new colours. Bar 10 will need a secure left hand in order to avoid accidents when hands are played together. If your pupil finds the first chord in bar 14 rather a stretch, the lowest note can be taken by the left hand – prepare for this by always playing F with the fifth finger in the three preceding bars.

The joyful mood returns with the replaying of the first section, and only the slightest easing of the tempo will be needed in the final bar.

B:1 Volkmann *Lied der Grossmutter (Grandmother's Song)*

Tender loving words of wisdom are delivered in this gentle song which needs a beautiful singing tone and an ability to accompany the melody sensitively.

The piece is divided into six, two-bar phrases; performing the slurring marked in the right hand not as literal slurs but more like violin bowing will preserve the sweep of the expressive melodic line. Together with your pupil you might compose some words to the melody in order that the natural shaping of the phrasing is felt. Given such a task, it is often revealing how creative and expressive young players can be. A golden singing tone on the right hand's top line will be encouraged by lots of separate-hands practice, and singing along with your pupils will help them absorb the shape naturally by ear.

The left hand is mostly in two parts, with a humming bass-line and an offbeat inner part (until bar 9) which gently fills in the harmony and keeps the movement flowing. This inner part is played with either the thumb or second finger and its dynamic must be kept down to a minimum so that the right-hand line can be heard above it. Take care, from bar 9 onwards, that moving quavers are not too intrusive. Dynamics do not rise above the *mezzo-forte* of the penultimate bar, but the hairpins indicate much rise and fall within a quiet range.

In bars 10 and 11 spread the grace notes in a leisurely manner before the beat, stretching the time over bar 11's top G♯, the highest note and the climax of the piece; after this, fall back into the flow for the rest of the piece, which reaches its conclusion in the warm and loving embrace of the final cadence.

B:2 Schubert *Two Waltzes*

These sophisticated waltzes, with their origins in the Ländler, conjure up images of the perfumed ballrooms of Viennese society. To achieve the elegance and lilt that this music demands, the player must be sufficiently dextrous to negotiate the playing of double notes (3rds in particular), as well as having a physical ease at the keyboard and reasonably large hands. This piece is therefore most suited to the older teenagers and adults taking Grade 4.

Both waltzes are in A flat major although their characters are slightly different, as is shown by the demands of the left hand. The athletic left hand of the first waltz combines leaps with large stretches. The second waltz has a more fixed left hand which for the first seven bars repeats a dominant pedal note under second- and third-beat chords, and when the bass line moves in bars 9–12 it does so in positions which are comfortably found under the hand.

The right hand holds the melody line in both dances. Given that dynamics are editorial, players are free to make their own decisions. In the first waltz, however, consider making an echo effect in bars 9–12, as this defines the harmonic sequence musically.

Separate-hands practice will be needed for these pieces to be well-balanced in sound quality. They would also benefit from being known from memory (even if not played from memory in the exam); this will allow close observation of the keyboard when making jumps and finding tricky chord-shapes, and ensure that the dancing lilt is maintained throughout.

B:3 Vaughan Williams *Valse lente*

Plenty of fresh country air is on offer in this slow valse, with more than a hint of the pastoral style often associated with English composers.

Minor outer sections are contrasted by a more sunny major middle section. Notice how the melody line is threaded through the texture, taken by left then right hand in turn, with parts dovetailing. The left hand sings the melodic line until bar 8 when the right hand takes over with quavers leading into the melody, again *cantabile*, in bar 9. The left hand takes the tune back, with the quavers that lead into bar 20; there is yet another handover at bar 24, this time with chords up to the top G in the right hand (bar 25) which leads the way until the *poco rit.* It is the middle part (right hand) that next takes the melody, in bars 33–9, with a bell-like descant line on the top; from bar 41 the final statement of the tune rings out boldly in the top voice before dying away to a quiet ending.

Textural clarity is important, and accompanying figures need to be carefully balanced so as not to interfere with the melody threads. In bars 33 etc. particularly, plenty of separate-hands practice will be required for the parts to be properly voiced. Here the use of the *una corda* pedal will add colour, but it should be lifted at the beginning of the crescendo in bar 40.

Judicious use of the sustaining pedal will enhance the singing sound. If put down with the chord in bar 50 and then held through the last bar's chord, it will increase the atmosphere at the end, leaving a memorable, haunting impression for the listener.

B:4 Carroll *The Reef*

This piece, one of the timeless character pieces written in the early twentieth century by Englishman Walter Carroll, remains a staple of the teaching repertoire because the writing is so perfectly crafted. The two lines of prose by Blood given below the title offer just the right imagery to capture a child's imagination, and are a good place to start when presenting this piece to your student. Full chords taking the player across the keyboard at the beginning illustrate the rock standing proud of the mighty sea, and the lighter passages from bar 4 etc. depict the waves which splash and surge towards the reef.

The indication 'Massive' allows your student to let rip with the sound in the first *fortissimo* and all subsequent ones. However, remember that the quality of tone must remain rich, supported by upper-arm freedom and the use of arm weight for the accented chords.

The clearly marked pedalling provides extra sonority. Supported by the pedal, the crotchet rests in bars 5–8 and 15–18 will allow the hands (first the left then later the right) to lift in order to find the third-beat chord in good time. In bar 22 the pedal should be held until the pause has been observed on the left-hand bottom C; it could then be effective to lift the pedal together with the hands during the rest, to give a small breathing space before launching into the last *fortissimo* phrase (this time played slower than at the beginning). Playing even more strongly in the last two bars – at *fortississimo* – brings the piece to a majestic climax in E major.

B:5 S. Heller *Study in A minor*

This spirited study will suit a deftly-fingered student who can get around the keyboard with ease. Almost a cross between an étude and a dance, it works best in one-in-a-bar – as the metronome mark indicates.

Dividing the beats, with triplets and quavers juxtaposed, often causes problems; rhythmic unevenness can be remedied if, from the outset, words are fitted to the rhythm. Teach the right hand separately at a slow tempo; use the words 'strawberry lemon cheesecake' to articulate the rhythm in bar 1.

The right hand's melody divides into two parts in the section from bar 9 onwards, where the triplet is followed by a minim on the second beat. The minim needs to sing for the remainder of the bar to achieve the *dolce*, and the bar's last three quavers should be treated as a little accompaniment to the minim. This suggestion of a lilting waltz style is reinforced by the *con grazia* marking at bar 37.

The left hand is mostly in a supporting role, but do not overlook its *marcato* in bar 29. For smaller hands to achieve the accent in bars 30 and 34, the left-hand Fs might best be played by the thumb. Accents abound throughout; in bar 1, for example, the left hand should have more of a pointed attack, while the accent over the right hand's first note should aim for a more lyrical sound.

Take care with the clef changes, firstly in bar 47 with the right hand in the bass clef, then from the second beat of bar 54 when both hands are in the treble. A build-up to the long right-hand E in bar 57 then fades away into the distance with a faint goodbye on the last two notes.

B:6 Schumann *Erster Verlust (First Loss)*

Taken from one of the greatest sets of teaching pieces, *Album for the Young*, this is an ideal choice for the artistic child. It expressively depicts the grief of one's first loss and needs a beautiful right-hand cantabile, an unhurried and spacious approach to the phrasing, and an ability to balance the hands carefully.

The slurring is clearly marked, but pay attention to the music's longer lines; for the most part the piece is shaped in four-bar phrases, with two-bar phrases between bars 17 and 20.

The *forte-piano* marked on the first upbeat (and in bar 8) should not be over-exaggerated, but should instead convey an expressive yearning. The right hand's dotted crotchets in bars 2, 3, 4 and similar should sing out, the left-hand notes tucking in underneath to fill out the harmony.

At bar 16 the first section can ease to a close, with spaciously placed left-hand octave Es. The writing becomes more complex from bar 17, so extra practice will be needed; when a piece's first section is easier and probably more practised, on reaching a trickier section a performance runs the risk of falling apart. Take care to hold the long notes of the left hand's lower line in bars 21–5; in particular, the crotchet B in bar 24 needs to be held through the D# to provide a solid bass to the dominant 7th chord. An alternative approach for small hands at bar 25 would be to take the right hand's minim G together with the left-hand E, using fingers 1/2. The outburst of anger from the end of bar 28 with the stamping *forte* chords gives way in the final two bars to reconciliation and acceptance.

C:1 Hoddinott *Leapfrog*

This is a refreshing and descriptive alternative so don't automatically leapfrog the piece if it is not immediately to your taste. Some may be put off by the unfamiliarity of the harmonic language, but this piece provides an opportunity to engage with a distinctive sound-world from almost 100 years ago.

Consider beginning work on this piece with a short improvisation; any notes are allowed but the music must vividly convey the 'Leapfrog' title, with plenty of characterful articulation, rhythmic playfulness and dynamic contrast. Comparing the end result with this piece and drawing on your students' imagination and ear for sound will help draw them in. Don't fail to mention that it is one of List C's easier pieces once the notes are familiar.

In preparation, each phrase must have a visual image or character portraying the title. Consistent and organized fingering will help the physical memory, but the melodic memory may take a little longer; begin slowly when learning the notes of the melody but include all marks of expression and dynamic detail from the first.

Clean and even articulation will help bring the semiquavers to life, but attention to the expressive detail is equally significant. Much of this will need to be bold and exaggerated to convey the effect. The small crescendos, staccato quavers and rocking left-hand quavers in the pedalled bars all add to the colour.

Since the piece also relies on rhythmic confidence, some rhythm work away from the instrument will reap huge rewards, whether tapping a table or having teacher and pupil clap one part each. It is on this rhythmic framework that the notes 'hang'. Ensure that the final bars are counted correctly, as anticipating the final chord will spoil the cheeky end.

C:2 Kabalevsky *Sonatina*

This deservedly popular piece probably rivals only the same composer's Toccatina in its popularity. It is superbly written for the smaller hand, presents lots of interesting musical challenges, and has a strong, playful personality.

Essential to its persuasive character will be the execution of the dotted rhythms, which must be both clear and decisive; any hint of a triplet will destroy the piece's character. Suggesting that the semiquavers belong to the next note will help – they should be tucked in, almost like a grace note. A light, neatly placed, rounded hand with fingers close to the keys will assist the articulation. The left-hand chords, achieved with active finger-tips and a spring from the bottom of the key, need to be similarly precise and crisply articulate. The little accents marked throughout are just brightness to the sound, to be created by a little energy from the finger, not by a robust push into the keys from the hand.

Another crucial element in a successful performance is a controlled sense of pulse. The piece relies on its rhythmic impetus and any slight unevenness will destroy the effect. Even at the end keep the pulse absolutely resolute, letting the rests do their job.

Overall a colourful range of dynamic will need to be encouraged and graded. Due to the single-line melody it is important in bars 7 and 31 not to start the crescendo too loud. There also needs to be a perceptible difference in dynamic and colour between the opening and the middle section from bar 17. The decrescendo beginning in bar 36 should not be too bold, however, as enough tone should remain to allow for the *pianissimo* in bar 41 and to give some definition to the final crotchets.

C:3 Gerald Schwertberger *Honky Tonk Piano Rag*

This cheeky and cheerful rag will appeal to all but the most serious students. Co-ordination and rhythm perhaps present the primary challenges, particularly in the second section which looks far easier than it actually is.

The first four bars are repeated three times throughout the piece, so conscientious work focusing on the co-ordination between the hands in these bars is very worthwhile. Slow practice is part of the answer but, to gain further independence, practising with left hand *forte*, right hand *piano* and vice-versa will reap huge rewards. Increasing the brightness and separating left-hand notes slightly will bring the passage to life and colour the character. Bars 5–12 are fairly straightforward, though a light, shapely articulation in the right hand works well and the chords of the left hand should be lighter than its bass notes.

Bars 17–24, in which most technical problems will arise, contain passages rather like patting your head and rubbing your stomach simultaneously. The small, syncopated accents need to be conveyed within a balanced hand, the touch fairly light. Controlling the energy in the fifth finger while keeping everything else soft will take disciplined, separate practice. The accent is not a 'push' but a quicker attack. Similarly, the 3rds in bars 21–4 will need attention so that they sound together and are just a little pointed.

The hands can then be organized together, but take it slowly. There is plenty of scope for confusion as the patterns change from bar to bar. Accenting the bar's main beats in both hands will anchor the patterns; reversing this, accenting offbeat quavers, will help finger independence. After this section there is a joyful return to the familiar opening, but a firm, steady pulse needs to be kept here and throughout the rest of the piece.

C:4 Bartók *Tanz aus Butschúm*

This haunting gypsy-like melody from a set of Romanian Folk Dances will entrance many of your pupils. It is absorbing in its melancholic use of the augmented 2nd, and a wonderful, exotic spell is cast by the melodic and harmonic interweaving of D harmonic minor and its dominant major.

By nature the melody is a piece of storytelling as well as a dance. It therefore needs space and time, accompanied by an elegant yet gently undulating left hand. Pedal, balance and an instinctive feel for (rather than literal rendition of) the rhythmic patterns are essential elements in this performance.

Bartók is quite specific in his markings for the pedal and it is vital to put them into practice early on. Pedal changes in bars 11, 15 and the final bar are deliberately slightly delayed to avoid a cluttered texture; these will work well providing that the phrasing of the first two semiquavers is clearly articulated. If the piece still sounds over-pedalled then the fault will almost certainly lie in the balance between the hands – not in Bartók's pedalling. Left-hand chords should be kept particularly light, though more warmth could be given to the bass notes.

The *molto espressivo* marking is significant for Bartók and gives licence for rubato. Expansive, expressive triplets are crucial but the dotted rhythms should be played exactly (not as a triplet), as these are part of the dance's character. The semiquavers should be spacious and unhurried.

Overall, the suggested tempo of crotchet = 76 seems a little fast even though it is slower than Bartók's timing of 35 seconds for the piece. However, keep the tempo broad enough to allow the full range of dynamic shape and colour to be explored.

C:5 Heather Hammond *On the Swing*

This lively and characterful piece has a real feel-good factor. With the right groove and the all-important solid awareness of the pulse, it is fun and satisfying to perform.

In the exam many candidates still play straight quavers in jazz-style pieces that are clearly marked 'swung'. Here there is the clear indication to play the quavers as triplets, and the swung groove is reinforced in the title; if this is the first time your pupil has explored swung rhythms some recordings will help show the way.

Beyond this, the essentials are a security and feel for the rhythms (a rhythmically solid left hand, in particular), and a range of colour to hold the listener's attention.

Initially treat the left hand independently of the right, practising it with an almost metronomic awareness of the pulse – as if it were a 'rhythm section' of piano, bass and drums. The bass presents almost a solo line in bars 4, 8 and 13–20 etc., and the touch here should be pizzicato, not too short but detached.

It is over this rhythm section that the melody works its magic. Despite the phrase markings, a fractionally detached touch will give impetus and rhythmic energy as well as a little more 'push' on the syncopated tied notes. The crotchet triplets need a more deliberate, bold approach, each note detached but full length – this will create an intense and expressive character.

One of the temptations to avoid is getting carried away with the dynamics in the middle section of this piece. Throughout it is vital that all melodic lines have a dynamic shape and that a lightness of touch is resumed in bar 20, a moment of cheek before the gradual crescendo to the bold ending.

C:6 Alan Haughton *Stephanie's Song*

This is a melancholy, charming song; a rewarding choice for the instinctively musical and imaginative pianist. However, it is best suited to those who have some experience of pedal and can balance chords within one hand.

The pedal is important yet not always as simple as it may seem. Many bars work solely with a change on the first beat. To avoid a conflict of harmonies in bars 1 and 3, however, the pedal will need to change on the second beat as well. In bars 7 and 15 the pedalling should change more often or perhaps not be used until the beginning of bars 8 and 16 respectively.

Repeated notes are a significant feature of this piece. Whether the opening melodic Bs are played with alternate hands or all with the right hand is a matter of personal choice. The other repeated notes are accompaniment figures, and need very careful handling if they are not to interfere with the melody; a decrescendo through them will match the decay of the melody. If in doubt, stop with the pedal held down at the end of the phrase (bar 4, for instance) and listen to the balance: if you can hear more of the left-hand repeated G than the melodic G then adjustment is needed. This all assumes that the melody is well projected; to do this it is worthwhile mastering how to voice the top note of the two-note chords in the right hand.

Couple this technique with a relaxed pliancy in the rhythm, and dynamic shading and contrast (preferably more than marked), and the piece will captivate and charm.

GRADE 5

School exams often become a serious threat to practice around Grade 5, so forward planning is helpful to ease the pressure. The preparation time for this grade will need to be longer than for the previous grades, but some light pieces that are quick to absorb will help to maintain enjoyment in playing while the exam work is being systematically covered.

A:1 Haydn *Vivace assai*

Haydn is known to have been an amiable, fun-loving man – qualities which are reflected in this cheerful piece. Notes lie well under the fingers, and the simple textures will allow most pupils to grasp the piece relatively easily.

There is a bright, happy quality to the first section, in which the music is propelled forwards by its characteristic detached two-quaver upbeat to each phrase. The right-hand 3rds need clear articulation, and slow practice will ensure really neat synchronization when the left hand plays semiquavers. Care should be taken not to rush bars 4–6 which may feel rather slow in comparison with the opening burst of activity. Sharply defined dynamic contrasts give variety to the sound, and keeping the left-hand semiquavers quiet will help to highlight the melodic line.

The change to B flat major for the middle section of this ternary structure must follow without any loss of momentum. Again, balance needs care, especially when the hands are playing far apart. Dynamics change frequently from bar 32 onwards and although a natural tailing-off will occur as the harmony resolves from dominant to tonic in the *forte* passages, any *forte* following a passage at *piano* should make a firm impact. Semiquavers slurred in pairs in bars 25 and 27 may seem fussy at this brisk tempo; candidates may prefer to play them smoothly, accompanied by a staccato left hand. Joining the bass chords in bars 33–4 and 37–8 (notice that the thumb Bb is tied) will contrast effectively with the surrounding detached notes, and the top notes of the right-hand 6ths in bars 43–4 can be slurred while the thumb shifts downwards.

Bars 57–68 serve as a bridge passage to the da capo (which should be played). The dialogue at the start requires equal clarity from both hands; the repeated chords at bar 64 lend an air of expectancy, especially if each group becomes progressively quieter; and rests need full value before the opening section returns.

A:2 Kuhlau *Allegro con affetto*

The contrasts between long lyrical phrases and rapid semiquaver passage-work in this movement provide the opportunity to show both musical sensitivity and technical prowess. Its structure – a modified sonata form with exposition and recapitulation but omitting a development section – means that much of the music after the double bar is similar, if in a different key, to the opening.

The tempo should be flowing yet sufficiently steady to allow control in the passagework. The *con affetto* (with affection) is established immediately if the right hand's line is tenderly and flexibly shaped. Careful listening will ensure the right amount of tone for the left-hand accompanying quavers; these may be pedalled, releasing on the final quaver of each group. Note that the ornaments should fit into the quaver movement and the double-dotted figure at bar 7 needs precision. A change of mood at bar 9 can be effected by incisive fingerwork with a carefully graded diminuendo, and using the suggested right-hand fingering in the following bar will keep the dotted rhythm crisp. The *delicato* of bar 13 needs smooth, tender phrasing with a firmly maintained crotchet pulse at the transition between quavers, triplets and semiquavers. Confident right-hand fingering is essential for bars 19–22 (the end of bar 20 is particularly tricky), and slow practice will help to synchronize the hands. Equality of all the fingers can be achieved by practising the right hand in different rhythms and with varying accentuation, and the thumb must move smoothly under the hand to avoid any bumps in tone. The marcato chords in bars 23–4 can be played either smoothly with pedal or slightly separated; either way, firm tone with a highlighted top note will give them importance and weight.

The remainder of the piece contains similar challenges; however, the rests in bars 35–6 need full length, and good control will allow the tone in the final bars to fade away.

A:3 Richard Jones *Giga*

This bright, cheerful dance with its compound rhythm will appeal to candidates who value neatness and precision in their playing. The ornaments are integral to the style and so must be included – a factor worth bearing in mind when selecting the piece.

The tempo will be governed partly by the phrasing demands and the optimum speed for ornaments, yet a sense of four-in-a-bar should always be present in order to convey the lively character. There is a considerable amount of right-hand movement around the keyboard which needs reliable fingering; bars 8–9 and 20–22 are potential danger spots. Learning the right hand initially without ornaments usually makes sense, however, the frequent changes of finger required to maintain clarity means that it is probably easier to incorporate most decorative figures from an early stage.

Clear fingerwork and phrasing are as important for a stylish perform-ance as good choice of tempo. Some initial scale practice using a finger staccato may be needed to sharpen up articulation; imagining the way a violinist or oboist would phrase the right-hand part may help to achieve the right amount of incisiveness. Most unslurred notes can be lightly detached: the two-note slurs in bar 1, for example, imply detaching the second and third of each group of three quavers. This will provide stylistic contrast with the bars that contain multiple groups of quavers slurred in threes (e.g. bar 9).

Keeping the left hand light and usually detached will add rhythmic momentum to the rhythm; the groups of quavers that link the right-hand phrases can have more prominence, however. Care is needed to hold the dotted crotchets in bars 8 and 13–14 for their full value in order to create a third voice in the texture.

A few main dynamic levels are given but within these broad bands the tone can be shaped as the pitch rises and falls. *Forte* implies a bright, harpsichord-like tone, and generally light offbeat notes ensure a spring in the step.

A:4 Handel *Ouverture*

The style of this majestic, joyful piece will best be assimilated by listening to performances of Handel's orchestral suites played on period instruments, while imagining the grandeur and majesty of life at Court.

Replacing two equal quavers with a dotted pattern is a characteristic rhythmic convention of the French Overture's slow introduction, and this performance suggestion is given at the foot of the first page. A slightly detached manner of playing will give definition to the rhythm, which must be consistently maintained here and in the final section. The mainly three-part texture needs the clarity of stringed instrument tone, mostly strong with a clearly projected top part. A slight drop in level at G minor in bar 9 adds musical interest, and sustaining the inner (second violin) line is especially important through the ties that create suspensions.

The central Allegro (which starts promptly at the change of time signature) needs a one-in-a-bar impetus yet without feeling so fast as to rob the music of its natural elegance. The canonic writing at the opening can be brought out by giving equal importance to both hands, and detaching most crotchets throughout the section will promote rhythmic buoyancy. A firm, bright finger action should give clarity and definition to the quavers, which may be played smoothly or slightly detached. One can imagine two oboes playing the 3rds in bar 30, perhaps with echoes at the repeats. Slow practice may be needed to ensure that notes sound exactly together, and using 4/1 to begin the more awkward D minor version at bar 37 will avoid the thumb on C♯. Momentum must not be lost at the ornaments, which may be treated as mordents. Despite a discrepancy of tempo instruction the last section recaptures the spirit of the opening; the final chord should be given full length and importance.

A:5 J. N. Hummel *Allegro in C*

Elegance and charm are in abundance in this sonata-form movement written by an underrated contemporary of Beethoven. Confidence will be required for moving around the keyboard, and although much of the mainly scale and arpeggio movement is in quavers, a few rapid passages (e.g. bars 32–6) might cause problems for the less agile player.

The time signature indicates crotchet beats but thinking two minims in a bar will help to achieve flow and momentum. A really secure pulse, which does not waver according to the demands of each section, is fundamental to the style. Bar 31 may need slow practice to ensure that the hands synchronize neatly, and care must be taken not to double the pace of the chords in the final two bars.

Clear articulation of the phrasing detail – such an integral part of this style – is dependent on responsive fingers and a flexible wrist. The opening four bars can be regarded as two, two-bar phrases, the slurs more akin to bowing instructions, whereas short slurs (e.g. bar 8) need a clear, yet not abrupt, lift in order to 'let the air in'. When trying to preserve natural accentuation, be aware that slurs do not always end on the weak part of the beat (e.g. bars 16–17). In bar 12 and similar, alternative fingering should be sought if the implied 4-5-4-5 proves troublesome for the semiquavers.

The main dynamic levels are indicated, but the natural rise and fall of the line will also be a useful guide to shaping the melody; a keen ear should ensure that the left hand always accompanies rather than dominates.

Sforzando notes need highlighting, and tone should build towards the end of each double bar. A spirit of restlessness pervades the central development section (bars 38–55) as it explores related keys. This lively exploration precedes a well-paced rallentando and pause to provide repose before the recapitulation.

A:6 Schytte *Allegro molto*

Candidates who like showing off their well-developed fingers will enjoy this instantly attractive piece. A sense of fun and character must be present throughout, and concentration and fluency will be needed to maintain the music's impetus as there are few, if any, real breathing spaces to gather one's thoughts.

The *Allegro molto* indication poses its own demands but the wise candidate will hold a little pace in reserve for the accelerando at the end. In music which has a natural momentum the tendency to rush can be avoided by periodic checking with a metronome; although a little flexibility is needed to allow the music to breathe, especially at transitions between sections, a firmly maintained pulse must underpin any performance.

Essential to this style is responsive fingerwork, which will be dependent on a good attack. A rounded hand position allows the tips of the fingers to be used, and a flexible thumb will ensure that no bumps disturb the flow. Practising the semiquavers in different ways (varying rhythms, accentuation, dynamics and speed) will help to secure the note- and fingering-patterns, some of which are slightly unexpected.

There are three main sections, with the third an exact repeat of the first, after which a coda based on material already heard rounds off the piece. It is important to maintain musical interest through clear phrasing and dynamics, as these are elements that are often under-characterized in the pressure of an exam performance. Really quiet tone where indicated allows a wide overall dynamic range to be conveyed, and use the accents to point the rhythm. The G major section with its strong tone and dotted rhythms provides an effective contrast with the neighbouring music. Definition will be given by detaching the accented crotchet chords, and the rising two-bar sequences will benefit from terracing dynamic levels. The left hand plays an accompanying role throughout, sometimes prominently (as in the accented minor-key bars of the first section) but more often lightly and gracefully.

B:1 J. S. Bach *Andante*

Here is one of Bach's relaxing, predominantly melodic slow movements in the manner of the ever-popular *Air on the G String.* This is perhaps not so surprising given that this Andante is a keyboard transcription of a string sonata.

Left-hand quavers can be played gently detached, as if pulsating, to support a seamless right-hand legato. In certain places the melody will necessitate finger substitution but where connection is impossible, pedalling is appropriate. For example, without the aid of the pedal it is difficult to link either the end of bar 10 to the beginning of bar 11 or the first to the second beat of bar 18. The latter may also be helped by fingering the semiquavers 4-2-1-2, thereby optimally positioning the hand for the next chord.

In bar 9 it may be useful to gauge a demisemiquaver speed mentally while playing the semiquavers in bar 8. If the demisemiquaver speed is correct, the hemidemisemiquavers are less problematic – although tapping exercises, moving from one note-value to its double, could also be valuable. Fingering the first two demisemiquavers with 2-1 avoids the discomfort of 4 and 5 when playing the hemidemisemiquavers.

The dynamic level seems restrained but the right-hand part should sing, perhaps at *mezzo-piano* rather than *piano*, especially in the rich tenor register at the opening. Semiquaver phrases need easing in, avoiding any hint of an initial accent and, where the writing is in parts, the dialogue can be demonstrated through varied dynamic levels for upper and inner voices. Modulations in the second half raise the musical tension: this may be reflected in a crescendo from halfway through bar 15 to bar 17, and then deflating to the cadence at bars 18–19. A slight crescendo, coupled perhaps to a very slight ritenuto, will anticipate the gentle shock of the minor at bar 24.

Although the Baroque era is rarely represented in List B, the obvious expressiveness of this Andante – perhaps anticipating Romantic expression – makes it an appealing inclusion.

B:2 Grieg *Norwegian Air*

The term 'air' could be interpreted as song or as the substance we breathe. In either case, this piece has a breezy, out-of-doors feeling that implies a clean sound and a crisply rhythmic energy. The suggested tempo is fast enough to yield an overall one-in-a-bar feeling, but clearly defined beats within this reflect the marcato specification at the top.

Reappearances throughout the score of the same musical material ease the learning task. The first eight bars are repeated twice, and bars 41–8 are a minor-key version of bars 9–16 (the same fingering will work for both).

Pedalling is determined by textural requirements, changes on first beats of the bar being suitable in bars 1–7 (and later equivalents), but with another change on the second beat of bar 8. Greater flexibility is desirable elsewhere. For example, pedal may be applied to the third beat of bar 9 and to the second beat of bars 10 and 12. The staccato chords in bars 10 and 11 need to be dry but not percussively abrupt.

Although no general dynamic level is indicated at the beginning, a healthy *forte* is sensed, holding *fortissimo* in reserve for the final bars. However, the initial *forte* needs to allow room for the *fz* emphases, which can be achieved by rotating the right forearm leftwards just ahead of the bar-line, before swinging fingers 5 and 3 down at the beginning of the following bar. Otherwise fingers should be active, dropping from a raised position to produce the necessary clarity, but only minimal arm-movement need be engaged.

The *una corda* pedal can be used to colour bars 25–48, although a more singing *tre corde* character from bar 41 may be appropriate. Throughout this section, the *fz* occurs within a *pianissimo* context so should be no more than a little 'peck'.

The guileless melodism and comparative straightforwardness of this piece make it an attractive – and safe – choice.

B:3 Schumann *Von fremden Ländern und Menschen (Of Foreign Lands and Peoples)*

There is a domestic appeal about this piece from Schumann's *Kinderscenen* ('Scenes from Childhood'). Perhaps the composer was dreaming of family life yet to come, imagining his beloved Clara playing this simple, idealized evocation of foreign lands and peoples to the couple's children.

The editor's metronome mark allows the music a natural flow but even a notch or two slower will do no harm. In keeping with the essential simplicity of the music, excessive rubato is not necessary, although the ritenuto commencing at bar 12 and the pause in bar 14 need to be significant enough for the examiner to be aware of their expressive function. Also, a slight easing of the tempo in the last two bars would not be out of place.

A light touch is called for, with the outer fingers of the right hand raised a little higher than the others to ensure a gentle projection of the melodic part. Care should be taken to keep the thumb as close to the key as possible to avoid ungainly bulges in the accompaniment figures. Textures will be enhanced by using the pedal, which can be changed on the beat – although pedalling through the whole bar is appropriate in bars 8 and 22.

Only a small dynamic range is necessary, but the melodic contours can be complemented by a subtle rise and fall to shape the higher notes of the two-bar phrases, perhaps with a slightly greater swelling into the second bar of the longer four-bar phrases. The transfer of melodic material to the bass between bars 9 and 12 should be emphasized; physical and musical energy will therefore need to be channelled down the outer fingers of the left hand, leaving the right hand largely to take care of itself (once learned).

A simple approach to this music is appropriate since much of its expressive charm lies in its understatement, and this needs to be reflected in performance.

B:4 J. F. F. Burgmüller *L'hirondelle (The Swallow)*

Although the title of this piece is *The Swallow*, its rippling character could equally well evoke a mountain stream. Whether we are in the air or on the land, the suggested tempo of crotchet = 108 allows the music to flow along without any sense of rushing.

Arm-crossing, the most obvious technical feature of this piece, may well challenge left-hand accuracy but, once mastered, the technique is visually impressive, almost always attracting admiring comments when skilfully executed! The left-hand part can be practised independently, but it is helpful to remember the harmony because nearly all the left-hand notes are harmonic extensions of the accompanying triads. It may be useful to memorize the biggest leaps, such as the one over bars 2–3, because visual contact with hands and keyboard can aid accuracy – but do be sure that your pupil knows where to look back to on the page. Loss of place after looking away from the score is a common cause of breakdown in performance.

Pedalling can be applied throughout, with around half of the bars needing one change to match the shift in harmony as in, for example, bars

1, 3, 5 and 7. Elsewhere, the pedal can be held through the bar; this will allow the texture an appropriate resonance, softening the left-hand staccato notes and guarding against percussiveness and angularity. *Piano* is the loudest marked dynamic although the rising contour of, among others, bars 2 and 6 is reflected by a gentle crescendo. The right hand should be kept very close to the keyboard, the fingers being lifted just enough to make the notes speak. The left-hand crossing motion can describe a shallow curve (rather like a phrase mark). This will ensure that, in places such as bars 2 and 4, the hand has moved far enough rightwards for three fingers to be strategically poised above the required triad.

A performance of elegance and harp-like resonance will beguile the listener – and the examiner.

B:5 C. Franck *Lento in C sharp minor*

Imagining an organist lost in an improvisatory reverie may give a key to the style of this piece. However, where the organist can use registration to voice the music, the pianist has to use touch and balance.

The piece is essentially a song for the left hand which occasionally enters into dialogue with the right hand's melodic fragments at points such as bars 6–8, 13–14 and 16–19. (Note that in bar 8, quavers 4 and 5 in the right hand should be played as F♯, not F✗.) The *forte* dynamic can signify 'full' rather than 'loud' because an expressive left-hand cantabile is required throughout. Using a deep, firm touch and a sense of near overlap from one note to the next can aid the necessary super-legato. Nearly all the phrasing outlines a rise and fall in register, and shading within the main dynamic levels can effectively reflect the phrase contours.

Use of the sustaining pedal will guard against textural aridity (which would be unstylish), but it is hard to generalize about its application. Sensitive listening to the harmony and texture remains the ultimate guide, but a few possibilities are worth mentioning. In bars 1 and 3 the pedal can be held through the bar, whereas only beats 2 and 3 in bars 2, 4, 5 and 6 need be pedalled together. Changes on every quaver in bar 7 will avoid blurring.

The rhythm seems straightforward, but at the slow tempo of crotchet = 54 it will be tempting to increase the pace at places such as beats 2 and 3 of the first and second bars. It may therefore be useful, in the preparatory stages, to count in quavers to ensure stability. The suggested tempo allows the music its necessary breathing space but is not so slow that an effective *rall.* is unachievable where marked.

If possible, ask a good cellist to play the left-hand part for your pupil: much can be learned about romantic *espressivo* from listening to the cello.

B:6 H. Hofmann *Ländler (Country Waltz)*

The country folk in this dance sound rather more like gentry than peasantry, the music seeming to call for some polish and elegance. A tempo of crotchet = *c.*120 can convey the lilt of the music while also retaining its pastoral character.

When playing double notes there will need to be a sense of channelling the arm weight along the outer fingers of the right hand to ensure melodic projection above the accompanying textures. However, from bars 10–13 (having observed the second-time bar) the melodic interest is transferred to the tenor register, so the musical and physical focus will need to be on the left hand, particularly the inner fingers which carry the upper melody. The octave oscillations above should be executed from a minimally rotating wrist, if these accompanying patterns are not to intrude.

Pedalling is desirable throughout, with changes on the first and third beats of the bar accommodating much of the harmonic scheme. However there are places, such as bars 4 and 5, where the pedal can be held through the bar, and the humour of bars 32–3 is probably best caught if no pedal is applied. Dynamics are generally unforced and a cantabile character maintained even when the music is marked *forte*; here weight can come more from a raised finger than a raised forearm. Responses to '*sempre cresc.*' along with '*string.*' and '*rit.*', specified in bars 26–31, should be significant if the examiner is to be made aware of them. The ritenuto can take the music to below the original tempo, and lingering on the final G of bar 31 will make the switch to *piano a tempo* all the more effective in the last two bars. As befits a dance, the tempo can otherwise remain fairly constant.

This music presents no huge technical demands, and a pupil with a good singing tone and sense of texture could create a charming interlude in a Grade 5 programme – and remember to include the repeat.

C:1 Mike Cornick *In the Groove*

The inclusion of music from the jazz or swing repertoire has proved popular over the years, and this attractive piece by Mike Cornick is bound to be a winner.

If your pupil has a flair for swing, there will be little or no difficulty with the rhythm, but there are a few traps for the unwary. For instance, at the start of the second phrase (bar 5) the rhythm of the first two bars might be expected to return, but instead the pattern of bars 3 and 4 is repeated. It is also a help to mark the places where notes or chords of the accompaniment actually occur directly on the third beat, as in bars 7 and 8. In the first of these bars the third-beat chord is weak (marked staccato and slurred); in the next bar it is stronger and sustained. Offbeat accents are an important feature of the style and should be clearly marked.

The composer indicates how the pairs of quavers should be swung, but remember that single quavers (upbeats) and chords that follow a quaver rest will still be in the triplet rhythm. In the early stages of learning, encourage the pupil to tap a steady crotchet beat with the left hand while playing the melody. It is not difficult and will improve co-ordination. Once hands are together, tapping with a foot or practising with a metronome indicating four beats in a bar will be a useful guide until the rhythm is safe. Thereafter, the music will flow better if it is thought of as two beats in a bar, at a tempo of minim = $c.60$.

In the exam the repeat should not be played, so the eye must get used to moving down to the second-time bar that lies directly below. Keep a really firm beat going through the last three bars so that the rhythm does not sag.

C:2 Tan Dun *Staccato Beans*

It is always rewarding to learn music from different parts of the world. This fascinating piece by Chinese composer Tan Dun will be enjoyed by those who have a spirit of adventure and an ear for special effects.

The staccato beans of the title may be jumping beans that the composer played with as a child, but the piece also conjures up images of a Chinese dance, with colourful traditional costumes, fluttering fans and the tiny running steps of the dancers. It is written in the pentatonic scale, which, together with the repetition of fragments and clashing chords, creates the very special Chinese sound-world.

The essentials of a convincing performance will be threefold. Firstly, the ability to keep the tempo (a brisk crotchet = $c.144$) in strict time right up to the final note; secondly, observing every dynamic mark from the *pianississimo* to the *fortississimo*; and, perhaps the trickiest of all, combining different articulations. Initially, separate-hands practice will help to establish the specific articulation for each part, and then slow practice together will allow time to ensure it remains accurate, even when the hands are making different movements. Anyone who has played Bartók's *Children's Pieces* or *Mikrokosmos* will know that this skill takes a little patience. Look out, too, for subtle changes to the articulation. The first ten-bar theme is repeated an octave higher, but in bars 21 and 22 the pairs of quavers, formerly accented, become slurred. Some passages (i.e., right hand at bars 22–3 and left hand at bars 34–41) require a semi-staccato touch.

The *sforzando* chords starting at bar 35 should sound like clashing cymbals, and at the *pianississimo* passage, *una corda* pedal will help with the sudden and extreme change of colour that is needed. The last few bars should be played by memory so that the maximum effect can be obtained from the crashing chords and athletic leaping across the keyboard.

C:3 Koechlin *En faisant un bouquet (Making a bouquet)*

The gentle, almost reverential mood of this intriguing piece brings to mind the style of a chorale or ancient plainsong. The title 'Making a bouquet' seems to suggest thoughts of affection for someone.

There are no time signatures, and almost every bar is a different length, but if thought of as a steady flow of crotchet beats there will be no difficulty. The only bars that do match are bar 3 and the last bar where the two main cadences occur. These should be felt in compound duple time with two dotted-minim beats. In addition, the very long first bar ends with a similarly shaped cadence.

The principal technical challenge will be to achieve a secure legato fingering. Excellent fingering has been provided and should be followed carefully, observing the finger substitutions (bar 2) and places where notes are taken by the other hand (bars 6 and 7). All should flow as smoothly as possible, with the exception of the slightly detached crotchets at the cadences.

Once the fingering is secure, legato pedalling may be added to enhance the tone. The pedal should be changed with each harmony, and the movement of the bass line provides a reliable guide. However, avoid pedal at the cadences; this will not only create a change of colour but will allow the tenuto staccato crotchets to speak. There is a natural rise and fall to each phrase with a more positive crescendo to the climax in bar 5.

However, even there it is only *mezzo-forte* and marked '*sost. ma dolce*'. The gradual diminuendo from bar 6 to the end will require careful handling so that the tone still has sufficient resonance at *pianissimo*. The *una corda* pedal would be useful in the last bar, adding a new colour; try to place a little more weight on the E of the final chord to bring a warm glow to the ending.

C:4 Saúl Cosentino *A la memoira de Astor*

The celebrated Argentinian composer Astor Piazzolla is famous for his exciting and colourful use of the Tango in his compositions. This affectionate tribute to his memory would be an excellent choice for those who enjoy sentimental music. For the busy teenager, it has the added attraction of containing only two eight-bar phrases, the first of which is played three times in all.

The performance instruction is '*Very slowly and with sentiment*', and while the given metronome mark may feel rather lugubrious, it should not be quicker than crotchet = 46 for fear of losing the nostalgic mood. Setting the right speed will be crucial. A good idea would be to sing silently the melody notes of bar 32 as a lead into the opening chords. Count the rests carefully in bar 8 (and similar); there is a danger of starting the melody too soon here.

The given pedal marks suggest that there is just one change per bar, and this can be made to work with careful balancing of the melody notes. For instance, in bar 3 play the semiquaver B♭ gently so as not to overpower the crotchet on beat 2. However, in bars 7, 15, 21, 25 and 31, where the melody revolves within a small interval, an additional change on the second beat may be preferred. An even clearer texture can be achieved by changing twice in all the bars where the melody comes to rest on a crotchet (bars 3 and 5 etc.).

The phrase structure, a mix of one- and two-bar phrases, flows naturally; one could easily imagine words being sung to its haunting melody. In the contrasting section at bar 19, the harmony becomes more chromatic, the emotion more overt. A stronger level of dynamics should be employed here, but play the poignant 'echo' bars (bars 22 and 26) very tenderly, as though remembering something special.

C:5 Prokofiev *La pluie et l'arc-en-ciel (The Rain and the Rainbow)*

If you have a pupil with imagination and a sense of adventure, then this is a piece for them. It is also short – a mere 22 bars in length.

The title will stimulate some discussion: which bars describe the rain, and which the rainbow? The final tempo may vary according to interpretation. Prokofiev does not provide a metronome mark so performances could differ widely, from a thoughtful crotchet = *c.*72 to a flowing (two-in-a-bar) crotchet = *c.*120.

Before beginning to play the piece, it would be wise to examine the notes closely. Many of the chords are clusters of black notes and these are contrasted with C major chords. Learning the shape of these chords and how they move one to another will build keyboard security. Indeed, this is a piece that could easily be learned by memory, right from the start. By studying just one or two phrases a week, it could be learned quite quickly. This will make the middle section (bars 9–16), with its widely spaced lines and leaping left hand, much easier to manage as the player can watch the keyboard.

Pedal should be used sparingly, either to assist with legato or for colour. In the middle section, the left hand should be practised with the pedal, changing on first and third beats. This will sustain the moving line of 3rds and help to negotiate the wide intervals. Remember that in piano playing, the shortest distance between two points is a curve! Encourage a relaxed movement, the arm rising and falling easily. In bars 5 and 7 it would be effective to hold the pedal throughout the bar, and legato pedalling will also be needed for the final cadence.

The composer has provided all the dynamic and articulation marks that are required; if they are scrupulously observed, the music will surely come to life.

C:6 Satie *Méditation*

If you are looking for something to stimulate a pupil's flagging enthusiasm, this could be the answer. A sense of humour and enjoyment of the bizarre will be essential, and some understanding of French, too.

Phrases of a satirical poem describing the various stages of creativity are distributed throughout Satie's piece: inspiration comes first like the wind and then as the Devil, giving the poor poet goose-pimples. Finally comes dyspepsia: 'a terrible indigestion of mediocre blank rhymes and bitter delusions'.

Although there is no time signature, the phrases fall naturally into multiples of four beats. The dynamics are very specific and should be noted carefully. The seemingly simple right hand, a continuous tremolo, creates a constant *pianissimo* background, and the challenge will be to maintain this quiet sound while co-ordinating the antics of the left hand. The tremolo lies comfortably under the hand and should be played with fingers close to the keys, with as little movement as possible.

The flowing melody, heard five times, suggests the poet's musings and in between are the various interruptions. In the second interruption (the series of 4ths), an easier fingering for the smaller hand would be 3/5, 1/4, 1/2. The arpeggio figure following the melody's third appearance will require extra practice to enable a safe shift into the long tied C chord. Starting with the thumb, practise just the last two quavers (D-A) and the chord. Once that feels comfortable gradually add more notes until the whole arpeggio flows easily.

Legato pedalling will greatly enhance the texture and colours. The pedal can be depressed even before the first *pianissimo* notes are floated and need not be changed until the third note (F♯) of the melody, and then again on the D, B and A. Continue changing with the harmonies and where melody notes would otherwise clash. However, several phrases will be more dramatic without pedal – the sudden attack at *Voici le Diable!* and the staccato repeated (B) quavers, for example. Towards the end when indigestion sets in, the pedal should be released with each rest (hiccup!) and depressed on the chord as the music fades.

GRADE 6

The challenge of Grade 5 Theory, Practical Musicianship or Grade 5 Jazz will be successfully over as work begins on Grade 6. The slightly different criteria for the higher grades, printed in *These Music Exams*, emphasize the need for the musical character, style and details to come across with conviction. Hopefully, by now your pupil's technical fluency will support these developing ideas, allowing more focus on expressive stylistic aspects.

A:1 F. Couperin *Les petits moulins à vent (The Little Windmills)*

The image of tiny windmills whirring round in the breeze provides ample scope for the imagination. This famous harpsichord piece requires not only lightness of touch and nimble fingers, but a relaxed technique to allow easy movement across the keyboard.

Ornaments are an important part of Couperin's style, and in the early stages of learning the piece it would be best to give them a definite rhythmic framework. The mordents (see bar 1 and the suggested realization) will fit neatly with the left-hand semiquavers. At a slow speed they will sound pedantic, but later when the tempo is flowing more, they will take on a life of their own. The trills at bars 6, 8, 11 etc. are accommodated more easily, with the exception of the one at bar 15 where there is a sudden leap. Even the suggested single appoggiatura could cause delay; all of these points will require diligent practice. At bars 37 and 44 a light acciaccatura can be slipped in without difficulty.

The little commas (bar 1 etc.) are merely 'breath' marks and should not delay the next beat. Quavers in these bars should be either slurred or played staccato so a break will occur naturally. In the left hand, quavers should be lightly detached and the descending octaves held but not quite joined.

No dynamic marks are given, but when this piece is played on the piano it will sound colourless without them. The harpsichord produces more body of sound in the lower registers, so it would be appropriate to crescendo the passage towards the end of each section, where the left hand moves downwards in octaves. However, bear in mind that the bass of the modern piano is very powerful and that the right hand could be easily swamped. Elsewhere use repetition and sequences to introduce contrasts and echo effects, encouraging your pupil to contribute ideas. With the dynamics confined within a range of *piano* to *mezzo-forte* and a moderate tempo of crotchet = *c.*92, this character piece will surely spring to life.

A:2 Mozart *Courante*

There is more to this rarely played Courante than meets the eye. It will suit the thoughtful pupil who enjoys exploring texture and harmony.

All the tricks of legato fingering will be needed to achieve the smooth, flowing lines of the three-part counterpoint, and the very first phrase contains several of these important finger manoeuvres. From the octave G at the end of the first bar, the next note (A♭) can be played with the fourth finger (instead of the suggested second) but changed to the fifth as the alto notes underneath are begun. The fourth finger is then free to play the F. Do not try to make the substitution before the thumb has played, or is at least in position over the C, for the fingers might slip. With the fifth finger now on the A♭, it will have to slide gently down to G in the next bar, and at the end of this bar the fourth finger will have to creep under the third in order to reach the crotchet D.

Sometimes the stretches involved result in two or more consecutive notes being played by the same finger; the golden rule then is to make sure that the other line is perfectly legato. This will cover any tiny breaks that may occur. Playing legato also includes using nuances to help the notes blend more. For instance, a crescendo and diminuendo on the passages in 3rds and 6ths in bars 5–8 will disguise the piano's inability to play a true legato line.

Look out for the beautiful canon between soprano (bar 9) and bass (bar 10). This needs to be carefully shaped and matched, and it would be effective to play the crotchets in bars 12–13 (and similar) slightly detached to mark the cadences. The harmony of the first half follows the conventional pattern of moving from the tonic key to the dominant, but the second contains some adventurous modulations, hinting at C minor, A flat major, D flat major, E flat major and F minor before turning back to the dominant at bar 31 and the home key for the final section. Dynamics could be more colourful for the modulations, but overall the mood is one of serenity.

A:3 D. Scarlatti *Sonata in D minor*

The freshness and lilt of this delightful Sonata will make it a popular choice. The tempo of dotted crotchet = *c.*72 results in a dance-like character, but also makes the synchronizing of the runs a third apart and the flourish in bar 24 quite a challenge on the piano. However, the metronome mark is only a suggestion: so long as the piece is felt as a lively two beats in a bar, there is no reason why it cannot be taken a little slower. What matters is clarity and technical control.

The choice of articulation is an important means of expression, so spend some time discussing this with your pupil. It was usual to play upbeat quavers in a detached manner, and the first note and the quaver at the end of bar 2 are good examples. At this *Allegro* tempo they will sound staccato. Appoggiaturas and suspensions must be slurred, so a search should be made to identify these. The first crop of appoggiaturas is in bars 5–7, where first- and second-beat quavers resolve gently on to the next quaver. The crotchet D in bar 4 and the tied notes in bar 19 are suspensions, and these, too, should be slurred to the following note. More can be found, and the search will be a useful learning process for the pupil.

Ornaments all fit neatly with the left hand and can either be played as suggested in the score, or as demisemiquavers beginning on the opposite note than the one indicated. In this case, the first one in bar 2 could last either through to the second-beat E or stop on the third quaver. Upper-note trills give a piquancy to the harmony, emphasizing the dissonance. In bar 17 (and similar) where the trill is on the lower note, fifth finger on A and fingers 3 and 2 for the trill may be easier than trying to trill against an adjacent finger.

As this is harpsichord music, dynamics are not given, but on the piano it is accepted that variety and colour are a necessary part of a successful performance. Again, your pupil should be encouraged to think of his or her own ideas – this way the ideas will more likely be remembered!

A:4 C. P. E. Bach *Solfeggietto in C minor*

The exhilaration and sparkle of this familiar piece has ensured its place in the affections of generations of keyboard players.

The natural position of the hands at the start of the piece places right hand over left, but for all subsequent overlaps (with the possible exception of bar 29) the opposite will prove to be the more comfortable. It will also ensure that the left hand does not start with a bump. Allow the right hand to drop downwards from the last note of each group as the left moves into position above.

Evenness of touch is clearly very important: the first six bars of the theme should flow seamlessly, relying on dynamics and nuances to give shape. Slow practice and then using different rhythms are just two tricks of the trade for developing finger independence and equality. For example, try either a dotted quaver, semiquaver rhythm or quaver then triplet semiquavers. In order to build up speed later, encourage your pupil to practise in short bursts, just a beat or two at a time, always resting and restarting on the first semiquaver of a beat. Gradually lengthen the groups until all flows easily and evenly.

In bars 7 and 8 a slight accent on the top note of each group will trace the melodic outline and create rhythmic buoyancy. Allow the hands to fall and rise gracefully over these pairs of notes. The wedges in bars 13–16 are a form of accent rather than staccato, so the octaves (*forte*) could be held for as much as a dotted quaver, while the 6ths (*piano*) are a little shorter. This lengthening of notes is a means of expression in early keyboard playing and is sufficient to give emphasis without resorting to accents as we know them in later piano music.

The piece reaches a climax at bar 30, heralding the reappearance of the principal theme back in the home key of C minor. As the last phrase rises and the texture thins out, a diminuendo is the most satisfactory way to shape the ending, and only a slight ritenuto is needed for the last five notes as the music fades away.

A:5 Clementi *Rondo (Allegro spiritoso)*

The freshness and high spirits of this Rondo will appeal to many players. It lies beautifully under the hands and has some exciting orchestral effects that bring to mind concerto form.

It would be helpful to listen to a Rondo by Mozart, especially one from a concerto in which the soloist announces the theme (K. 488 or K. 466, for example). Hearing the interplay between soloist and orchestra will suggest ideas for this Clementi movement. For instance, the first eight bars are relatively quiet (soloist), and then repeated louder, with some thickening of the texture (orchestra). It would be fun working out with your pupil what happens thereafter.

Staccato marks appear in several places, but almost all quavers should be lightly detached, saving legato for those more expressive ones marked with slurs. Pedal will enhance several carefully chosen passages: bars 20 and 21, changing with the Bmin-Dim7-Emin-Amaj harmony; and 31 and 32, where a short pedal on the first quaver of each group of three will add emphasis to the descending bass line. Passages in which the bass notes appear as dotted crotchets (see bar 46 and similar) will also benefit from pedal. Here the composer is indicating a more lyrical and sustained texture. If preferred though, the pedal could be released for the three repeated melody notes in bars 46 and 48 to give just a little more character.

Assure your pupil that there is nothing to fear from the extended trill that rounds off the middle section. It can be played in semiquavers, running on naturally from the preceding bars. This may sound rather pedantic at first, but once the piece is up to speed (at about dotted crotchet = 76), it will make a respectable flourish. Of course, the more confident players can employ a fast, free trill if they wish. Whatever is chosen, the trill will need a triplet inserted just before the two final notes to round it off neatly. Count the dotted crotchets carefully in bar 62 – they might be shortened – and remember to keep the *poco rit.* going through the rests after the trill in order to maximize the impact of the joyful return of the Rondo theme.

A:6 Telemann *Vivace*

This is a piece for those who love to feel their fingers running. The music abounds in repetition and sequences so there is ample scope for echo effects and terraced dynamics.

In keeping with its high spirits, the quavers should be played staccato unless they are included in groups of slurred notes. At bar 18 (left hand) hold the long tied note with the thumb while detaching the quavers underneath. The few crotchets that occur (e.g. in bars 18 and 19) should be given some length, if not full value.

The left hand spends much of its time providing the supporting pulse and harmonic structure, and you could imagine this played by a cello. However, there are two passages of semiquavers (beginning at bars 14 and 35) that will require some extra practice in order to negotiate the intervals and shifts confidently. If the given fingering does not suit, spend a little time working out something more comfortable. For instance, if the first group of semiquavers begins with the second finger, the second group with the fourth (or occasionally third), and the third group with the fifth, a finger sequence is established that suits all the bars involved. It is much easier to remember and also gives greater technical security.

In a few passages the editor has suggested that some semiquavers should be held on, either by inserting small crotchets against the notes (bars 6 and 31) or by adding quaver tails (bars 10 and 28). This is a harpsichord device that helps to enrich the texture and give greater prominence to the selected notes. At speed it is not easy to play the passages with added quaver tails, and it works just as well if those notes are given a little more tone and the repeated thumb notes less. The crotchets are much easier to manage, especially if only fingers 1 and 2 are used; the use of 3 on the C (bars 7 and 32) puts undue strain on the other fingers, so just tuck the thumb under instead.

A tempo of crotchet = 92–100 will be quite sufficient to give brilliance and zest to the performance.

B:1 Beethoven *Adagio*

It is ironic that the hardest part of this delightful and poetic slow movement is not in fact written by Beethoven but by Donald Tovey! Apart from bar 35, however, there is little difficulty in the notes themselves, but this is only a small part of the story. For example, the art of keeping the semiquaver accompaniments harmonic yet in the background will require much subtle control, patience and listening.

Avoid using any pedal at first; instead, aim to achieve a clearly defined melodic line in the right hand and harmonic warmth with the fingers in the left. Playing the bass notes of each left-hand figuration 'over-legato' will help this, and even in bar 3 create a gentle, descending cello line from the lower notes of the pairs. Above this seamless accompaniment the right hand should sing its melody with plenty of musical shape and length of line.

The transition from semiquavers to sextuplets in bar 9 needs careful handling. There should be no abrupt 'gear-shift' nor should the tempo slow. A breadth of tempo is important, however, to give space to the figurations, so ease them in by holding back a little through the left hand's repeated As in bar 8. Balance is harder to achieve here, with so much movement in a high register, so the dynamic contrast between the hands needs to be quite extreme (probably more than the performer believes necessary); this will be achieved with a pliant wrist and perhaps fingers flatter and closer to the keys.

Bar 33 to the end will need particular attention both technically and musically. An eloquence of shape in bar 34 is required; allow a little more time in bar 35 to avoid it sounding panicked. Make an expressive statement in bar 37, leaning a little onto the first semiquaver of each group with delicately placed left-hand chords and a gracious, feminine ending.

At times throughout the piece a hint of pedal would be appropriate, but given the risk of using too much it is best not to plan it but to judge by ear. The pedal should rarely if ever be fully depressed: instead use light dabs to pivot the damper and allow the sound to blossom.

B:2 Chopin *Moderato*

This is a beguiling piece with beautiful shifts of harmonies and a captivating melody, which is entrancing in its unpredictable phrase-lengths.

Put aside immediately any idea that this is a sort of march; any suggestion of this will spoil the overall character and mood. To avoid clumpy and intrusive offbeat chords there has to be a subtlety of balance in the left hand. This can only be achieved by preparing the sound well in advance, so quick and assured movement from the bass notes is needed.

It is easy to be *laissez-faire* with the fingering of the chords and bass notes but organizing which fingers play what will be crucial in developing good control. Practising with the eyes shut will ensure that there is some physical freedom and confidence to the jumps. The chords then need to be 'floated in' with a light hand while an imaginary cello, supported by the pedal, conjures up a smooth, slightly more prominent bass line.

Within the right hand the melody should sing through even when it is the top note of chords such as in bar 3. Refined voicing here and elsewhere will reap musical rewards. Practising the piece with no pedal will help challenge the fingers to produce a legato and musical line. Be aware that the right hand's semiquaver rests are not there to provide a hiccup in the melody but are a reminder to the performer to observe the dotted rhythms carefully yet within the legato phrase inferred by the phrase line. The pedal should change with every bass note (first and third beat), helping to blend the harmonic movement.

Even with a carefully judged and balanced texture there is still the danger that the piece could sound robust and driven, so an instinctive sense of rubato is also important. Bar 2 cries out for just a little time at the end and Chopin's arpeggiated chord in bar 4 even more so. Put the chord's grace note before the beat and its lowest note (G♯) together with the left hand.

Explore a more insistent sound, fractionally urgent and bolder in the middle section, before relaxing at the end of bar 13 into the repeat of the opening.

B:3 Stenhammar *Molto tranquillo, semplice*

This is a delightful piece, full of warmth, love and compassion; for the musical pianist it will be a compelling choice. It sounds so simple and uncomplicated throughout, and the performer should capture this. But don't be fooled! In order to convey its personality, the piece does demand a subtle control of sound, a refined awareness of and sensitivity to balance within a one-handed chord, and the most beautifully judged pedalling.

Begin by organizing the fingering clearly to enable as much of the piece as possible to be legato; this will necessitate a certain amount of substitution. It will be important to practise with no pedal at first. Aim to achieve with the fingers a seamless line in the 3rds underneath and throughout the melodic quavers – adjust the chosen fingering if necessary. The consistency of this fingering will enable each finger to have the exquisite control needed to voice the top line gently. The repeated crotchets at the opening also need just a little more projection than the 3rds – which, as the moving part, will be heard in any case.

More elusive still will be the chordal patterns from bar 13 which should perhaps be viewed as shifting and shapely harmonic lines rather than melody. Again, a slight voicing of the top notes and an overall shape to the phrase is needed. As before, aim to achieve this subtlety of sound and line without pedal at first.

The pedal changes must never be abrupt and should instead gently blend the harmonies. Changes on the first and third beats in the opening bars and on every beat in bar 4 would be appropriate, and in the middle section change with every shift of harmony.

The *dolcissimo* towards the end cries out for the evocative, dreamlike quality of tone that can only be coaxed from the piano by using the *una corda* pedal – this will enhance the sleepy and content ending.

B:4 Glière *Prelude in D flat*

One quick look at the quaver movement in this entrancing Prelude is enough to realize where the dangers lie. In a musical performance this attractive piece will conjure up the happiest of memories, yet in the wrong hands it could sound Toccata-like, lacking melodic direction and subtlety of colour. It is often the case that the greater the technical demands, the less we should be aware of them; the controlled and musically shaped quavers in this piece will require a lot of disciplined practice yet should be unobtrusive in every way, just providing a water-colour backdrop.

The secret lies in deciphering what is important, spotting the hidden melodies and harmonic patterns; to some extent the suggested pedalling will help. The opening two bars, for example, sweep up to C then float down to A♮ above a beautifully disguised and unexpected F major harmony. The top notes provide a melodic line, under which the broken chords should be dynamically shaded, matching the decay of the upper notes. Glière points out where the melody needs to sing even more eloquently above the quavers: a little more weight and tone is needed here to shape the tune.

Balance issues are compounded in the middle section from bar 25, in which a projected left hand should be entirely independent of the right-hand quavers. Before adding the right hand some separate work with pedal will be needed to give the melody its control, shape and sense of line.

While your pupil must be technically in command of the tonal colours and blending, the piece may still sound rather mechanical without a sensitive use of rubato to help convey the phrases. Freedom of time should not be overdone, but it is important to have a little easing-in of the tempo and slight relaxation at the ends of the longer phrases. It may well help to pencil in the longer phrase-lengths to help see the musical direction.

Use the dynamic range to the full but be aware of the piece's limited texture and range; avoid anything too forceful, therefore, allowing just a little leeway for the delicate *pianissimo* at the end.

B: 5 Liszt *Klavierstück in A flat*

Not typical Liszt, and almost Brahmsian in its waltz-like character and general lack of chromaticism, this elegant piece is captivating, with the most spine-tingling of harmonic shifts towards the end.

The most ravishing of repertoire often comes at a cost, however, and this piece is not easy. The balance between the melody and accompaniment figures in the right hand will need careful attention. In bars 3 and 4 etc. the accompaniment figures will be technically a little awkward to play under the melodic notes, and uncomfortable stretches suggested in bars 1 and 2 may need substitution for smaller hands. It is absolutely vital that the melody sings above the right-hand quavers; this requires complete independence of fingers. A lot of patient, slow work with the right hand is needed: evaluate the balance and tone on every note and remember the 'feel' of achieving the right sound so that it can be reproduced at will.

There are some rather awkward jumps in the left hand, which should be measured and remembered so that the hand can travel to its notes with the player barely glancing down. With so much to respond to and think about musically there will be no time to tell the fingers where to go in performance. Fortunately the pedalling is quite straightforward. Changing on the first beat of each bar works well but this will depend greatly on the balance between melody, bass and accompaniment; a responsive ear and fine adjustment to the instrument is crucial at all times.

Once mastered technically, the performance will need a musical sense of rubato, perhaps moving forward to bar 3 then taking a little time to suggest the accented 3rds rather than giving them a bold push. The performer will also need an innate understanding of just how to colour beautiful moments. For example in bar 21, a little time taken beforehand is essential to anticipate and lead the listener to the magical shift to F flat major (enharmonic E major). The performance will need dynamic subtlety both here and over the poignant 3rd in the penultimate bar; the Cb is a fleeting suggestion of minor tonality before a reassuring perfect cadence in A flat major.

B:6 Schubert *Allegretto in C minor*

In order to relate to this somewhat moody piece it's worth remembering the days when you wake up feeling decidedly grumpy. Even with a brief sojourn into E flat major and C major, Schubert can't really shake off the gloom of the first section of this Allegretto. The Trio is more of a thoughtful interlude, perhaps evoking memories of happier times before the self-centred irritableness sets in again.

There are only a few awkward moments technically. The 3rds in bar 29 should be singled out for attention, and bars 9–17 will need a seamless fluency as the canonic writing gathers in intensity to the unison *fortissimo*. The *ffz* quavers are easier to play if not too angular and snatched; think of them as a shouted two-syllable word, full of anger, given its due emphasis and time.

The main challenges are musical. The broad dynamic range should be communicated without the tone becoming too strident in the *fortissimo*.

Shapely quaver movement and a true legato will help shade the opening and a delicate, well-contrasted *pianissimo* is needed for the reassuring major reply. Just a dab of pedal with a gentle release is all that is needed here.

The canon following the double bar should also be nicely legato, and build urgently to the *fortissimo* without an accent on the first notes of the phrases. A small ritenuto into the pause may help the drama. More important will be to give the bar's rest its full value and in bar 20 to allow plenty of time for the pause – the gloom has time to lift before the opening theme returns, now in C major.

The central section presents a risk of sounding very disjointed. Writing in the longer phrases will give a visual sense of the musical direction, and tonally balancing the chords to the top note will give a sense of line (though in bar 47 the balance shifts to the lower notes). The pedal might follow the couplet phrasing here, going down with the first and up with the second lighter chord.

The piece tells a story, so from the very first note your pupil should not just include but interpret Schubert's markings, telling the audience something about themselves and the music.

C:1 M. Arnold *The Buccaneer*

With its boisterous good humour and predominantly loud dynamic level, this piece is not one for the faint-hearted!

In general the notes lie comfortably under the fingers, however, clear articulation will be the key to an expressive performance. In bars 1–2, and at equivalent points later in the piece, your pupil may find it expedient to remain on finger 4 in the right hand and 2 in the left when playing the sixth quaver. The tempo of the music does not exceed the comfort zone for achieving the necessary repetition through wrist action, which also complements the *fortissimo* dynamic.

Bold rhythms but with a hint of playfulness are required to bring the music to life. The hemiolas in places such as bar 11 (beats one and two) and especially in bar 17 need care. A pupil/teacher clapping duet could be a helpful preparatory exercise, with the pupil clapping crotchets to the teacher's quavers (emphasized as in 12/8), then to the teacher's dotted crotchets. Once mastered, the effect should sound natural rather than contrived. The 'tum-te, tum-te' rhythm in, for example, bars 7 and 8 suggests an energetic spring with a pronounced up-and-down motion of the forearms, as if choreographing the rhythm.

The dynamic markings are mostly *fortissimo*, but it would be wise to open the music at a level which leaves something in reserve for the most strident moments such as those at bars 13–15 and, perhaps, at the very end. Accents need a sharp attack, descending from above with the full weight of the arm – beauty of tone need not be a concern here! At bar 8, the *forte* could be treated as a full-sounding *mezzo-forte*, in preparation for the tune in the bars that follow. Where *pianissimo* is specified, the effect can be aided by using the *una corda* pedal, perhaps inserting a slight diminuendo in bars 32–3 to maximize contrast with the ensuing *fortissimo* outburst. There is no real need for the sustaining pedal although its use may enhance the textures in bars 35–8.

The character of this music is 'larger than life' and it needs to be played with confidence and swagger – it's definitely a good choice for the noisier pupil!

C:2 O. Peterson *Jazz Exercise No. 2*

Despite the perhaps uninspiring title, this piece is an attractive, sparkling introduction to jazz piano by one of its great masters. Although fully notated, it can act as a model for more personal explorations by the aspiring jazzer.

The adopted tempo should yield enough momentum for the music to come to life, but the nimble fingered can happily take it to a crochet = 128 (or above), bearing in mind the quicksilver character of Peterson's own playing. Whatever tempo you opt for, mastery of a good fingering in the preparatory stages – as with classical studies – is essential. There are some helpful suggestions supplied but in bars 9 and 10 you might like to try fingering the 3rds 3/2-4/1-5/2-2/1-3/1. There are also places where hands may helpfully be redistributed. For example, in bars 18, 20 and 22 the left hand can play the triplet at beat 3 (in addition to that at beat 1), then take beats 3 and 4 of bar 24, and the D-C#-C♮ of the following bar. As with all passages requiring hand-swapping, it is a good idea to practise the moment of transfer in isolation to ensure rhythmic precision.

Quavers need to be swung and, to preserve stylistic consistency, passages notated as dotted rhythms will require the same treatment. The shorter note may sometimes be slightly emphasized to guard against too 'classical' a definition of the metre: at places such as the second beats of bars 8 and 16, the phrase can end quite abruptly, thus highlighting the syncopation.

There are no dynamic indications but the music needs energy without heaviness. A discreet *mezzo-forte* would be a suitable basis for the first sixteen and last eight bars, allowing scope for some rise and fall and offbeat accentuation. The 'middle eight' (actually a middle nine!), bars 17–25, can generally be quieter, perhaps with a preparatory crescendo in bars 24 and 25.

Although stability of pulse is essential, a literal approach should be avoided to allow scope for personal touches that complement the style. To get an idea, listen to Peterson himself playing, for example, *Lulu's Back in Town*. And don't be disheartened by the brilliance of what you hear – even he had to start somewhere!

C:3 Satie *Gnossienne No. 3*

One theory has it that the name 'Gnossienne' was inspired by dances from the Cretan town of Knossos (or Gnossus). Given Eric Satie's interest in the occult, the idea of a slow, mystical choreography may provide a clue to the character of this piece.

Your pupil does not need to be put off by the score's lack of bar-lines because the music can initially be learned in 4/4. However, in performance, over-awareness of such a framework would probably miss the point because the melodic parts need a sense of freedom, as if floating above the left-hand accompaniment. Rubato will enhance the music's expressive effect if applied at appropriate points. For example, longer melodic phrases can incorporate a slight accelerando followed by a ritenuto, perhaps starting and ending a little below tempo before restoring the basic pulse in the exposed left-hand parts.

A very legato approach is desirable all the way through, ensuring that the first of any pair of repeated notes is held down for as long as possible. Pedalling is essential and also straightforward, since pedal changes need only occur with the left-hand bass notes. The dynamic remains essentially *piano*, with the right-hand tone projecting a little above that of the left. Nuances are also necessary, however, to reflect the melodic shapes and the magic of the composer's sound-world. Where a hairpin crescendo/diminuendo is marked, this needs to be heard, and it may be useful when practising to exaggerate the effect before moderating the dynamics to levels more appropriate for performance. Additional gentle mid-phrase swellings can be incorporated into, for example, the second and fourth right-hand phrases and similar places later in the score. Where Satie has written *enfouissez le son* (muffle the sound) above the last line, use of the *una corda* pedal is a helpfully colouristic response.

Other cryptic comments written into the score probably reflect the composer's eccentric sense of humour and need not be taken too seriously. However, *conseillez-vous soigneusement* (consider carefully) implies a thoughtful manner, perhaps slightly below tempo in the fifth melodic phrase, and where Satie writes *très perdu* (very lost) the tempo could be very flexible – as long as it is not so erratic that it sounds like miscounting!

C:4 Poulenc *Staccato*

Bucolic jollity pervades this staccato march, which is full of the composer's characteristic sense of fun. One can imagine it scored for wind band, perhaps featuring a dialogue between solo clarinet and solo flute in bars 17–24. The piece is an attractive option, not least because repetition of material reduces the task of learning.

This is not to imply that challenges are lacking and without a crisp, rhythmic staccato it is hard for a performance to convey the musical character successfully. The secret is in the wrist action which needs to be taut (though not tense) and springy, rather than loose and floppy, supported by firm finger-joints. When learning the staccato chords, it may be useful to practise the lower 3rds as well as the upper melodic part independently, paying particular attention to the 'bounce' needed for clear articulation of the semiquavers (a sensation that can be practised on a table-top). With familiarity, the sensation can be imagined ahead of execution – it is surprising how far skilful technique relies on being mentally prepared. The semiquaver chordal repetitions should also be accommodated by the tempo, so the indicated metronome range seems sensibly *Pas vite*.

The *très sec* textures require no pedal (with the possible exception of bar 17), but dynamics can be strongly contrasted, so that the *forte* at bar 17 comes as a real surprise to the listener. Up to about bar 36, accents can be thought of as emphases rather than attacks; thereafter much more force can be brought to bear. The accents from bar 41 to the end can be harsh and percussive, executed in a sharp downward motion from quite high above the keyboard. In fact, bar 32 to the end can be thought of as a continuous crescendo, but your pupil will need to have something in reserve for the final *fortissississimo*. Neither ritenuto nor rubato is appropriate – note the composer's injunction not to slow down near the end – and even the commas in bars 20 and 22 need last no longer than it takes to draw breath.

This music is fun both to play and to listen to, and, if you're really lucky, it could put the examiner in a good mood too!

C:5 Mark-Anthony Turnage *Tune for Toru*

The rather empty-looking score of this piece mirrors the sense of stillness that a sensitive performance can create and which was characteristic of music by the work's dedicatee, Toru Takemitsu.

The main problem technically concerns chords of a wide spread in the left hand, and the music, as written, may need adapting for small hands. In bar 9 the left-hand C♯ can be taken by the right, and a rapid *arpeggiando* can aid execution of the chords in bar 11. In bar 14 none but the largest left-hand span can encompass the G to E 10th. Two solutions suggest themselves. The first involves (unhurriedly) releasing the tenor G in favour of the lower notes, thus losing the G when the pedal changes – a shame, but sometimes unavoidable! The second solution is to change the pedal with the G, a quaver earlier than marked, sustaining the note to the end of the bar. This produces a slight harmonic smudge but, as the pedal is changed two beats later, the offence is minimal.

The shifting metres require care. Where the music moves to 5/8 it is useful in the early stages to establish a frame of reference by counting this and the surrounding bars in quavers. A feel for the triplet crotchets (bars 12, 22 and 24) may be developed by focusing on the steady 2/4 pulse and placing the triplet notes strategically around this anchor.

Dynamically the piece is generally subdued and, even where the composer writes *forte*, restraint is sensed. However, the music's contours can be reflected in a subtle dynamic rise and fall, and the marked phrasing may be taken as a guide to the application of such nuances. Phrase marks do not imply any musical disconnection, an otherwise seamless right-hand legato being broken only by the rests.

It is helpful to set an appropriate atmosphere before starting to play, sitting quietly in readiness for a few moments, mentally establishing the slow pulse, the body relaxed and at ease. The mood is therefore set before any notes are sounded, and it is equally effective to hold this mood for a few seconds, hands poised above the keyboard, after the last notes have died away.

C:6 Villa-Lobos *Rosa Amarela*

A clue to the character of this Brazilian folk-song arrangement surely lies in its title. *Rosa Amarela*, a beautiful yellow rose, suggests that the music needs to be played affectionately, the gently swaying syncopations enjoyed.

The piano writing demands no great dexterity from the pianist but it does require a good sense of textural balance, ensuring that the melodic right-hand part is not swamped by the full-voiced left-hand chords, which will need some restraint in terms of dynamic level. Pedalling is certainly called for, and in the opening and closing sections it can be changed with the harmony. Between bars 6 and 30 changing every half bar works most of the time, but greater restraint may be appropriate in the second half of bars 15 and 23 to achieve clarity in the left hand.

Adopting the metronome mark of crotchet = 72, or even a little slower at crotchet = *c.*66, allows the music an easy-going, natural flow in which the syncopations can achieve their full effect. To capture the underlying Latin feeling, right-hand rhythms should be nicely pointed, with semiquavers perhaps tending towards shorter rather than longer durations in the main melody from bar 6. The rumba-like rhythm in much of the left-hand part needs a firm placement. Counting out a semiquaver pattern 1-2-3, 1-2-3, 1-2 may be a useful preparatory exercise in developing appropriate rhythmic emphases within a stable framework.

Villa-Lobos has not written many dynamics into the score other than accents. The *sforzandi*, though not percussive, can be achieved simply by dropping the two outer fingers from a slightly higher position above the keyboard than is required for the surrounding notes. To add further interest, bars 22–9 could be thought to echo bars 14–21, with the former played at a healthy *mezzo-forte* and the latter a gentle *piano*. If the examiner is to be made aware of the hairpins in the opening and closing bars, your pupil should realize that effective dynamic projection sometimes involves a certain amount of exaggeration.

The music is attractive and not especially demanding technically for the grade. It is likely to be a hit with most pupils as well as a safe choice.

GRADE 7

The final grades should be equally rewarding not only to the pupils but to the teachers, parents and mentors whose support and involvement in the exams should be bearing much fruit. The playing usually sounds quite accomplished even at a pass level, while merit and distinction categories will acknowledge musical and polished performances of real artistic quality. The highest marks most frequently go to candidates choosing pieces within their own technical comfort zone, so that expressive details and communication can lift the music off the page.

A:1 J. C. F. Bach *Allegro assai*

This bold but good-natured music demands disciplined fingers, rhythmic stability and a well-sustained momentum. A tempo of dotted crotchet = *c.*72 generates an appropriate one-in-a-bar feeling, although a slight lean into the downbeat of every other bar conveys the mainly two-bar phrase structure, which is expanded into a four-bar design at places such as bars 13–16. The tempo requires little, if any, modification other than perhaps at conventional points of closure such as bars 31–2 and 123–4 where a *poco ritenuto* may be appropriate.

   The brisk character of the movement suggests a crisp, clear articulation with a strong sense of the finger releasing the key. Crotchets and dotted crotchets can mainly be held for their notated duration, but quavers benefit from a staccato touch throughout. Semiquavers should be connected if not played exactly legato. Slow staccato practice will be useful in developing the necessary precision, especially where the passagework is played hands together. In this regard, working on scales with hands a 6th apart may be a useful preparatory drill – and has the added advantage of anticipating the Grade 8 scale syllabus! These articulations keep the textures appropriately dry, requiring no pedal work as a result.

   Good fingering, such as that marked in the copy, needs to be absorbed if fluency and accuracy are to become habitual. Care will also be needed when preparing bars 41–8, which have the potential to become uneven. The sensation of a seamless passage from left hand to right needs to be cultivated, so the two semiquavers at the point of transfer can be practised slowly, firstly in isolation, then within their immediate context until the whole sequence becomes naturally flowing.

The few dynamics present in the score suggest that Bach is still thinking in terms of 'terracing' (i.e., nothing is indicated between *piano* and *forte*). The modern pianist need not be too inhibited by this and can allow volume levels to reflect the natural rise and fall of the musical contours. For example, dynamic interest can be achieved between bars 33 and 60 by starting the passage *mezzo-piano*, then initiating a crescendo at bar 53, reaching a healthy *forte* by bar 60. Earlier a subtle crescendo/diminuendo can effectively colour the alternating-hands passage at bars 41–8.

Despite some demands made on dexterity and co-ordination, the technical challenges of this piece are relatively modest, and its cheerful, uncluttered character makes it an attractive option.

A:2 Haydn *Allegro di molto*

As with the other Haydn sonata movement on the Grade 7 syllabus, this cheerful piece contains a significant amount of repetition. The musical design is essentially monothematic with the central episode developing the main theme in the tonic minor, so the amount of learning comes to rather less than three pages!

A tempo of crotchet = *c*.104 provides sufficient momentum to meet Haydn's *Allegro di molto* specification, but is not so fast as to render the passagework unmanageable by a Grade 7 player. With no obvious need for any modification, the opening tempo needs to be held steadily throughout, with perhaps just the suggestion of a ritenuto at the very end.

Semiquaver passagework should be even and precise, executed from active fingertips; to avoid undue percussiveness, it is best conceived in phrases. The left-hand 3rds in bars 115–18 are challenging and may be played lightly, with a freely detached touch and a spring in the wrist. Failing all else, there is no great crime in fully sounding the first and fourth of the 3rds, playing only the upper note of the intervening semiquavers.

The frisky character of the major-key sections can be realized by playing most quavers lightly and detached except where indicated otherwise by the composer. A more sustained feeling is sensed in passages such as those at bars 6–7, 13–16 and equivalent places, where discreet touches of pedal may enhance the texture. The minor-key section (bars 31–61) invites a generally legato approach. Indeed, this change of sound quality for the central episode helps to define the overall musical structure for the listener.

A mainly subdued dynamic level seems appropriate and, in the first section, only one significant crescendo need be applied, between bars 24 and

27, to be followed by a slight diminuendo. However, there is plenty of room for dynamic nuances within the greater scheme. The opening eight-bar phrase, for example, may be played with a slight crescendo and diminuendo to and from bar 5 – a pattern that can be applied to similarly structured phrases later on. In the minor-key music, a dynamic level of *piano/mezzo-piano* is generally suitable, although a crescendo feels appropriate between bars 39 and 41. From bar 108 onwards, a more boisterous attack brings the music to a sturdy conclusion. Where Haydn writes *fz*, emphasis within the context of the surrounding dynamic is implied, rather than a brutal attack. The purpose of the direction is to encourage projection of the offbeat phrasing rather than to make the examiner jump!

A:3 D. Scarlatti *Sonata in F minor*

The sparkle and brilliance often associated with Scarlatti's keyboard music is altogether absent in this minor-key sonata, which finds the composer in an unusually sombre mood.

Crotchet = *c*.84 allows the music a natural, lyrical flow which is probably best realized by a predominantly legato approach. For a smooth delivery, finger legato is essential, and the many printed specifications for finger substitutions and thumbs on black notes are necessary if melodic connection is to occur. If the use of thumbs on black notes is not to cause unevenness, the hand will need to be positioned slightly forwards on the keyboard. Forearms and wrists should be held as still as feasible, allowing the fingers a deep, sustained touch which needs to be very even. Evenness of legato can be practised in the context of a scale where the ear must be alert to the matching of sound quality from one note to the next. However, judicious use of the pedal can also help to preserve the legato in places where the texture thickens such as bars 17–21, 32–3 and 44–6.

Left-hand ornaments are best played on the beat, but fingering them with 1-2-1-2 may suit some hands better than the printed suggestion. Leaving aside questions of authenticity, the bass-clef notation in bars 62 and 63 can be effectively realized on the piano by playing a spread chord, F-A♭-B♭-C-F, placing the upper F on the downbeat and holding, rather than re-sounding, the lower F. The very last note of the piece can comfortably be played by the left hand, since the fifth finger will already be strategically placed.

Where the texture is polyphonic rather than chordal (as in bars 1–15), it is a good idea to project the top voice (indicated by upward stems) dynamically slightly above the inner voice, so that the examiner can follow the part-writing. More generally, dynamics can reflect the accumulation and release of musical tension. For example, a crescendo from *piano* can commence at bar 16 and peak at bar 22, before a diminuendo leads back to *piano* by bar 28. A touch of discreet rubato could also be included to reflect the interrupted cadence at bars 25–6. An even more sustained accumulation of tension may be sensed from bar 40 which reaches considerable intensity (if not necessarily immense volume) by bar 53, after which the music gradually deflates to reach a subdued ending.

This sonata is suitable for the serious-minded pupil whose hands are happier overcoming problems of balance and co-ordination than those of athleticism.

A:4 J. S. Bach *Prelude in G*

If familiar with Glenn Gould's recording of this prelude, you might perceive its tempo as a racing *prestissimo*. For Grade 7, however, the calmer approach adopted on the ABRSM CD may serve as an appropriate model. A metronome mark of quaver = *c*.132 yields an adequate tempo, although a nimble-fingered pupil can comfortably increase this to quaver = 144. Scrambling and loitering should both be avoided if musical flow and clarity of fingerwork are to be achieved.

To this end, close attention to fingering in the early stages of learning is essential, and suggestions printed in the recommended edition should suit most hands. Where there is potential for hand collision near the beginning, it may help to keep the left hand under the right in bar 2 and the beginning of bar 3, reversing this during the ensuing quaver rest so that the left is over the right for its next quaver G. Hopping octave quavers in the left hand can be played staccato, but adjacent quavers such as those played by the left hand in the second half of bar 4 and by the right in bar 5 seem to invite a more legato touch, giving these passages a melodic role. Mixed articulation works in bar 7, where the C and E quavers on beats 1 and 3 may be played detached and the intervening quavers legato. Generally the semiquaver triplets benefit from lightness of touch with a sense of releasing the key rather than lingering on it. Staccato practice can help to achieve the necessary physical sensation, ensuring that the fingers are active but the movements economical. Clarity is paramount if your pupil is to capture effectively the inherent dialogue of the two-part texture.

When played on the piano, it is probably appropriate to interpret Baroque keyboard music in terms of the piano's rather than the harpsichord's capabilities. To avoid a relentless effect, the natural melodic rise and fall of places such as bars 5 and 9 can be projected via a slight crescendo and diminuendo. It is also effective to play *piano* from midway through bar 13, then increase the dynamic during the rising sequences to reach a modest climax at bar 16. An extended diminuendo can take the music to a quiet conclusion, perhaps with a slight ritenuto just before the final chord.

This music may have been conceived as a prelude to a fugue but, in an examination context, it can present a fresh, sparkling prelude to a Grade 7 programme. Perhaps for your pupil it will be a prelude to discovering other gems from the *Forty-Eight Preludes and Fugues*.

A:5 Handel *Allegro in D minor*

Although Handel's keyboard music is less celebrated than Bach's, this miscellaneous Allegro shows how engagingly and idiomatically the composer could write for the medium. The challenges presented by this music are well worth overcoming; the solemnity of D minor perhaps needing to be counterbalanced by a fleetness of manner to avoid undue gravitas. A metronome setting of crotchet = *c*.96 seems well suited to the task.

The piece is not strictly a fugue, although it has fugal characteristics and typically demands clarity of part-playing. For example, the opening right-hand subject may need greater projection when it is transferred to the left (as in bars 7, 9, 17 etc.), as lower sonorities can be more difficult to detect by the ear. It is also helpful to define the musical subjects by means of a consistently applied articulation which can act as a structural cue for the listener. The opening right-hand subject should be clearly enunciated, perhaps with connected but not overly legato semiquavers. The secondary left-hand subject, first heard from halfway through bar 3 to the beginning of bar 6, may benefit from a generally staccato touch, but with legato third- and first-beat quavers. A similar scheme can be adopted when this subject reappears. Care will be needed with fingering patterns which are not always obvious, especially in places such as bar 16, and in bars 20–23, where using 2 for the final right-hand semiquaver of each bar will aid a smooth passage into the semiquavers of the following bar.

Occasional tempo modification and tasteful use of dynamics can add to the performance's character, resulting in a flexible rather than a mechanical effect. Cadence points can be reflected by an infinitesimal easing of the tempo, but the dramatic interrupted cadence at bars 36–7 seems to call for a more substantial ritenuto which may be extended to prepare for the concluding Adagio. A gentle dynamic rise and fall can be applied to places such as bars 3 and 4 where emphasis is directed towards the middle of the bar. A more general crescendo from bar 24 through to bar 27 seems appropriate, followed by a steep diminuendo to reach the F major cadence at bar 28. The Adagio ending is grandiose and the arpeggiated chords may be aided by use of the pedal.

Examiners will enjoy performances which present a clearly voiced musical continuum, successfully balancing the dramatic elements with the more playful, lighter moments.

A:6 Haydn *Finale (Presto)*

The fast speed and rhythmic game-playing of this movement suggest a good-humoured scherzo character – but with a touch of urgency. On first glance, the piece may seem fairly long, but Haydn's unusually economic use of the material means that there is nothing new to learn after bar 85.

Metronome settings of dotted minim = *c.*92–100 yield an appropriate tempo range enabling the music to be felt as one- rather than three-in-a-bar. The offbeat *fz* markings seem to undermine a clear sense of metre, so it is important that your pupil plays these in relation to a very regular pulse and an awareness of where the downbeats actually fall. (Perhaps the annoying 'ping' of a metronome has its uses in this context!) This way the listener may be teased – by design rather than by accident – until the *fz* accents in places such as bars 18–23 confirm the true metrical design of the piece.

Haydn writes no dynamics into the score other than the ever-present *fz* and some accent marks. This suggests an underlying dynamic of *piano/mezzo-piano*, otherwise the accents are unlikely to be very effective – although they need not be hammered! However, there are places that invite further dynamic response from the pianist. During bars 32–3 and 94–5 the chromatically rising music suggests a crescendo in preparation for the dramatic pause over yet another *fz* chord, which could effectively be followed by a *subito piano*. It might also be a good idea to commence the descending arpeggios at bars 41 and 103 at a healthy *forte* but gradually make a diminuendo before reintroducing the main theme at bars 46 and 108 respectively.

A technical feature of the piece that might be new to your pupil appears at three places where the right hand is required to play legato parallel 6ths (with an occasional octave). Using the printed fingering, it is possible for average-length fingers to join either the upper or lower note of one 6th to the upper or lower of the next – and sometimes both notes can be joined. The succession of intervals can be practised very slowly while mentally and physically concentrating on the connecting sensation. This sensation should be remembered when the music is brought up to speed, and will be assisted by a flexible, mainly lateral motion of the forearm and wrist, but with enough lift-and-drop to ensure articulative clarity. Discreet pedalling may also be used to aid a smooth delivery.

A successful performance of this music will need sustained momentum and projection of its good-natured drama.

B:1 Fauré *Andante moderato*

The melancholy beauty of this piece will make it a popular choice. A confident pedal technique, sensitive response to rubato and harmonic colour will be essential for a successful performance.

In this style of music, it is always worthwhile practising the left hand and pedal together before adding the right hand. The pedal indications here, in common with most editions of the period, are misleading to say the least. If followed exactly they would result in gaps in the bass line and smudges. However, pedal is required throughout the piece, beginning with the rising arpeggio figure of bar 1. As a general rule, it should be changed with every new harmony so that a firm bass line is created. Initially this means first and third beats, but in bars 6 and 7 it will be the first, second and third beats, and then every beat in bar 8. Similar pedalling will continue throughout the piece until some longer pedal effects in the last few bars.

For ease of execution, the rising arpeggio figure that starts each phrase can be shared between the hands, the left hand playing the first three or four notes. The melody rises and falls in expressive curves, and this should be reflected by dynamic nuances. In bar 8 the single semiquavers on the treble stave are part of the accompaniment and should be much quieter than the melody notes an octave above. In bar 9, the spread chord will need careful timing. As soon as the right-hand thumb has played the semiquaver F✖, begin rolling the left-hand chord, taking care to change the pedal early enough to catch the bottom note. Meantime, the right hand must hold the crotchet F✗ during the pedal change and then play the octave G♯ along with the left hand's B♯.

The second section (*dolce*) begins tenderly, but soon becomes more passionate as the music rises. An important enharmonic modulation occurs in bar 13 (notice that the minim G♯ is tied to the crotchet A♭) and from this point the tempo can be urged forward a little until the climax is reached at bars 16–17. Then a gradual unwinding of tension can restore the original tempo and create a mood of repose for the final section at bar 21. Here a tonic pedal underpins the texture and the harmony changes from minor to major. Take plenty of time over the last three bars, enjoying the warmth of the final chords.

B:2 Grovlez *La sarabande*

The poems of Tristan Klingsor that inspired all the delightful pieces of this set are also a rich source of inspiration for the performer. Here, the poet conjures up a ballroom scene from the past, describing the frills of the dresses and delicate shoes of the dancers. Like other haunted ballroom scenes, it fades away like a dream.

The elegant melody should flow easily, and care must be taken to ensure the correct rhythm. Practising with a metronome or with the left hand tapping a steady crotchet beat will help in the early stages. Later it should sound as though improvised, but underpinned by the steady, swaying left-hand accompaniment. Violins are mentioned in the poem, so imagining that sound will help to colour this first theme. The form of the piece is Rondo (ABACA + coda) and, in contrast, the first episode at bar 13 is bold in character, with the Saraband's characteristic second-beat accents strongly marked.

Pedal is essential in this piece, and it would be helpful to practise it with the left hand alone before adding the melody. In the first section it should be changed with each moving bass note: i.e., bar 2 – A, bar 3 – G and F♯, bar 4 – E and A, and so on. For the different texture at bars 8 and 9 use only a short pedal for the first quaver so that the staccato chords are clearly heard despite the *pianississimo* level of tone. The scale in bar 10 belongs to the sound-world of the first section, so it would be appropriate to resume the pedalling. As this is a rising scale with a crescendo, it will not sound blurred as long as the pedal is changed on the next two beats. At bar 13 pedal will add a rich sonority to the chords, but lift it at the commas to allow a tiny gap before the strong second-beat accents.

The second episode appears at bar 26, and it will be important to keep the thick accompanying figures murmuring quietly in the background so that the melody can sing clearly above. Here the pedal will need to be changed on every crotchet beat. The final appearance of the 'violin' theme is *pianississimo*, and the *una corda* pedal should be depressed throughout the last page. In the closing bars, as dawn is breaking, the clock strikes, and 'with tiny steps . . . the Saraband dancers slip away'.

B:3 Mendelssohn *Andante espressivo*

The *Songs without Words* contain some of Mendelssohn's loveliest piano music. In this one, despite its *Andante espressivo* heading, there is an underlying restlessness created partly by the rests that break so many of the phrases, but also by the accompaniment that urges the music forward.

Before settling down to practice, time must be spent deciding just how to divide up the recurring pattern that forms the accompaniment. The choice will depend on the size and shape of the hands. A simple method, which is helped by the layout on the page, is to take the four semiquavers of the second and fourth beats with the right hand. Skill will be needed to keep these notes quieter than the melody, and sometimes the stretch involved will impede an easy flow. In these cases (i.e., bars 13 and 18) all but the last semiquaver should be played by the left hand. This allows ample time for that hand to move back to the next bass note. Alternatively, this idea of playing most of the semiquavers with the left hand can be used in all but bars 26–8, 30–32 and 36–7 where the left hand has more to do. The advantage of this method is that it allows the right hand more freedom to shape and give singing tone to the melody.

The first section closes quietly in B minor at bar 10, but then the pitch and passion begin to rise. The bass line moves up in chromatic steps and the melody in sequences, building to a climax in bar 17 where the first theme reappears in C major. Practising the bass line (just the minims on first and third beats) with the melody will help to judge the balance of this passage with its gradual crescendo. Similar practice will also help with the third melody at bar 26 where the bass begins to move about more.

Once the balance of melody and bass line has been assessed it will be easier to add the rippling inner accompaniment. It must never be allowed to swamp the other two lines, and fingers and arms should remain as relaxed as possible when playing these notes.

Pedalling is essential but relatively uncomplicated. For most of the time legato pedal changes occur on first and third beats, thus sustaining the bass line, but between bars 26 and 32 changes must be more frequent. In bar 38 pedalling stops briefly to allow the rests to be heard, and then the principal theme resolves peacefully in the closing bars.

B:4 Chopin *Mazurka in A minor*

Because they look deceptively simple, Mazurkas are often among the first pieces of Chopin attempted by pianists. The best way to discover their special characteristics of rhythm and rubato is to listen to recordings by recognized Chopin specialists.

This beautiful example is nostalgic in mood, but with a more vigorous middle section that perhaps recalls happier days and the joy of dancing with a loved one. It will be this section that presents the most technical demands, and it is often a good plan to tackle the difficulties first.

The left hand is relatively simple, but the slurs from second to third beats should be clearly shaped. Devise a fingering that allows safe and easy movement across the keys so that the attention can be focused on the trickier right hand. Here the dotted rhythms must be crisp and energetic, becoming almost skittish in the *scherzando* figures (starting at bar 37). Mark the accents firmly in this passage, especially when they appear on third beats. Bar 44 will require some extra attention and courage in execution! Practise the left hand first, noticing that the thumb replaces the fifth finger as it lands on the octave F♯. Encourage your pupil to negotiate this manoeuvre without looking, so that the right hand's more daring leap can be watched. This section is often played at a quicker tempo than the outer parts, giving greater emphasis to the change of character.

The theme of the opening section has two distinct moods, and adopting a slower tempo of crochet = 120 (rather than the faster tempo marking indicated) will allow for expression and rubato. The first four bars are melancholy and persuasive, but the livelier answer becomes almost impetuous with a sudden quickening of tempo in bar 7. In order to time accurately the triplet semiquavers in bar 3 (a written-out turn), begin by playing six straight quavers (D-C♯-D-D♯-E-B) and then fit the triplet into that framework. From bar 21 feel the music urging forward until it broadens triumphantly into the reappearance of the first theme. Little or no pedal is suggested in most editions, but it is essential for colour and style. However, the frequency with which the pedal is changed will vary according to harmony and melodic detail. There are also moments where breaks in the legato pedalling will give greater clarity to the articulation, add shape to the ends of phrases (bar 4, for instance) and simply help the music to dance.

B:5 Schubert *Scherzo and Trio (Allegro vivace con delicatezza)*

Schubert's last piano sonata is one of the landmarks of the piano repertoire, but from this light-hearted, vivacious movement one could never tell how much searching and loneliness are expressed in the work as a whole.

Nimbleness and delicacy will be essential for a successful performance, together with an awareness of harmonic colour. It would be useful, then, to play through the accompaniment in block chords to discover the chord progressions and modulations, and to assist note learning. When played up to speed, it should murmur gently in the background. Indeed, the dynamic level for the whole movement is predominantly quiet, rising to *mezzo-forte* only towards the end of the first section (bar 77). Always confine accents to the dynamic level of the passage in which they appear. For instance, in 35–8 there are accents on all first beats – the *forte-piano* being just a little more pronounced than the more common accent of the preceding bars – but all are within a quiet phrase.

There are three pairs of bars (a fourth is a repetition of the first) that would be worthwhile memorizing. These involve sudden jumps that if not entirely confident will cause delay or accidents. They are bars 7–8, 15–16 and 83. The acciaccaturas should be on the beat, so at first your pupil could practise playing the ornament and principal note together, the hand dropping lightly onto both notes. At bars 21–4 the inner melody must be legato so a reliable fingering is needed. Try using the thumb for both appearances of C and G; the other fingers will automatically fall into place. This fingering also works for bars 29–32.

The Trio is a mysterious, rather macabre dance, and in view of its brevity, examiners will not mind if repeats are played. The right hand carries the melody, sometimes heard in the lowest notes of the chords, sometimes at the top. The articulation of two sustained minim chords followed by two slightly detached crotchet chords sets up a hypnotic rhythm which is heard as three minim beats across every two bars. The left hand then sounds like a restless offbeat punctuation, its accents incisive but not loud.

Familiarity with the layout of the complete movement will be essential to avoid confusion in the exam room. Omit the first-time bar altogether (bar 90), and round off the first section with the second-time bar. After playing the Trio, the first section is repeated (da capo) and the piece concludes with the third-time bars marked 'Coda'.

B:6 Wagner *Lied ohne Worte (Song without Words)*

A piano piece by Wagner must be one of the most surprising items in the syllabus. This *Song without Words* is very beautiful, not unlike the music of Franz Liszt, but with something of the operatic style of Bellini.

It is always worthwhile examining the texture of a piece before beginning serious practice. The three main strands (upper melody, sonorous bass line and inner chords) will require different amounts of tone. Initially these components can all be practised separately. Then it will be helpful to play the melody with the bass line so that the ear gets used to the balance. While the bass notes should never overpower the melody, some have to last for a whole bar, so they must sing sufficiently. The melody is full of suspensions, and while the dissonant notes are often marked with accents, they should be leaned on with the weight of the arm rather than struck.

Time spent practising the left hand with pedal will also be beneficial. Remind your pupil that, unless great care is taken, the sustaining pedal will create a build-up of sound as the inner chords are reiterated. Encourage a light touch and constant listening in order that bulges in the line are avoided. Only when building towards a climax should the chords be allowed to swell, and even then the melody and bass lines must dominate.

The dotted quaver, semiquaver figure should be taken literally, with the semiquaver placed just after the triplet group and thought of as an anticipation of the note that follows. There are a few instances of two against three (bars 7, 11, 12 etc.) that may need some extra attention, especially when the quaver-crotchet-quaver rhythm appears, but there are very few real technical problems.

At first glance the structure appears quite ordinary, with almost all phrases four bars in length. However, in the fourth bar of most – instead of the expected long note and feeling of repose – Wagner adds linking material that carries the melody forward into the next phrase. The mood of each link is different, but they are all operatic in character. For instance, at bar 4 the extra notes are purely decorative, while at bar 8 the repeated B helps to broaden the ritardando and acts as preparation for the change of key; at bar 20 it is persuasive, and at bar 24 urgent, as the theme sweeps on in octaves.

The suggested metronome mark of crotchet = 66 provides a suitable basic pulse against which the ebb and flow of this passionate music can pull.

C:1 Joanna MacGregor *Lowside Blues*

The funky style of this piece makes it an instantly appealing choice for candidates who enjoy exploring the crossover between classical and jazz idioms. Some interesting pianistic challenges are posed (not least of which is some heel tapping in a couple of places), and the composer's performance indications provide helpful clues to interpretation.

The hands need independence throughout in order to produce often opposing phrasing, and slow practice will help co-ordination in places (bars 9 and 19, very similar but not identical, are particularly tricky). In the repeated left-hand two-bar figure which underpins the piece, swagger can be achieved by firm thumb accents slurred to the next quaver, and clear staccato. Bars 3–20 contain two main right-hand phrases, each starting quietly and building to a *forte* which must be matched in enthusiasm by rhythmic heel taps. The semiquaver figures in bars 7–8 need clear attack, especially at their accented starts. In addition to the pedalling marked, substance can be given to the bass octave in bar 9 and elsewhere by a short 'dab' of pedal on the first beat. Note that the accidental (sharp) on the C in the right hand applies throughout bar 6.

Rotating from the thumb to the fifth-finger side of the hand will aid clarity in the grace notes and accented 4ths at bar 21. Light yet incisive tone here contrasts with the previous bar, and the downward patterns which follow should be detached, using a hand staccato action and the suggested fingering. In the bars in between, with their interplay between the hands, rhythm must not be distorted. An exciting surge of sound can be produced if the crescendo does not start until bar 29, as marked. At the end of this bar and through the next the right thumb needs flexibility as it moves between C and F (repeating the movement while the fifth finger holds the higher-octave C may prove beneficial), and an accent on each note will give excitement to the climax. Time is suspended for the delicious mixture of sounds to be enjoyed in the pedalled glissando at bar 31; it may be played using second fingers, with hands beginning a semitone apart.

The *a tempo* must be instantaneous, however, with all dynamics clearly projected and a tremolo that is free (i.e., not having a measured number of notes). The repeated *pianissimo* figure at bar 36 played at three different octaves sounds delightful if the tone is really delicate with no accents. *Una corda* can be used here and for the subtle, *a tempo* ending.

C:2 Ravel *Menuet sur le nom d'Haydn*

It is characteristic of the precision-loving Ravel to choose to mark the centenary of Haydn's death with a piece which makes a play on the letters of that composer's name in as many different ways as possible. An eighteenth-century elegance pervades the rhythm and phrasing, but in all other respects the piece is pure Ravel.

Notes need a careful eye at the learning stage, especially bars with many accidentals (bars 38–41 in particular), and numerous ties across bar lines must not be missed. A large hand-span will allow the often wide stretches to be negotiated with ease, but examiners will be sympathetic to candidates who need to omit the occasional unmanageable note.

The characteristic third-beat openings to phrases create forward momentum, while the accents can lend ambiguity to the rhythmic shape if surrounding beats are kept light. The numerous slurs often appear to separate phrases into small units, but thinking in longer 'sentences' of four or more bars will give a feeling of continuity and progression. A sense of one-in-a-bar should always be present even at this measured tempo, and rubato must be subtle and within the bounds of French good taste.

The opening five-note motif, which is repeated many times in various different guises, forms the backbone of the piece. Voicing needs clarity to project these phrases, especially when they appear in inner parts, and although the texture is often chordal there should always be a clearly audible melodic line.

Ravel's distinctive and wonderful harmonic language is to be enjoyed. His skill as an orchestrator is well known; imagining, for example, a cor anglais playing the tenor line at bar 19 and muted strings for the *pianissimo* chords at bar 38 adds more possible tonal colours to be explored. Frequent use of hairpins leaves the player in no doubt as to the overall dynamic shape – it ranges from *pianissimo* to the main *forte* climax at bar 27 as the music reaches F sharp major.

The pedal plays a vital role in sustaining bass notes and adding resonance to the harmonies. At the beginning of the piece, releasing the pedal at phrase-ends helps to define the rhythmic shape, contrasting effectively with the longer, more sustained lines later on. Some compromise needs to be reached between sustaining bass notes which cannot be held for their full length by the fingers and preserving harmonic clarity; the ear is always the best guide as to how long to hold the pedal before harmonies become a blur!

C:3 Bartók *Finale (Allegro vivace)*

Bartók's lifelong fascination with the folk-tradition of his native Eastern Europe is nowhere more apparent than in this lively peasant dance. In the score the composer documents every detail of phrasing, tone, accentuation and tempo variation, each of which needs careful consideration.

The piece comprises two main sections followed by a coda cleverly combining ideas from both parts. The first section (to bar 36) begins with a four-bar 'scene setter', the syncopated drone of which immediately evokes the sound of a rustic band. The eight-bar phrase in the right hand appears three times, each appearance different in character due to changes in accompaniment, register and dynamic. This phrase needs clear, controlled fingerwork together with an absolutely meticulous sense of rhythm. Right-hand thumb notes are often tied, and the carefully differentiated accents, *sforzandi* and tenuto marks each require their own level of attack within the mainly *piano/mezzo-piano* dynamic range. Good lateral movement of the hand enables the left hand to span the increasingly wide stretches which accompany the second phrase at bar 12. In the final appearance of the phrase some pedal highlights accents as the crescendo from *piano* brings the section to a decisive end.

A gradual return to Tempo I (bar 45) from a slower speed at the change of key heralds a new, more light-hearted mood, perhaps as a different group of dancers joins the merrymaking. The left-hand repeated figures at bar 39 can be fingered using the thumb on either D or E and the fifth-finger notes need prominence. Right-hand accents fall on the second beat in bars 45, 47 and 49, and the left hand will achieve lightness in its trill-like figure by keeping close to the keys. Soon, however, the balance shifts as the left hand takes centre-stage at bar 53. Right-hand staccato marks at bar 59 imply a slight fifth-finger accent, and the left-hand 6ths need precision and ever-increasing excitement. The pace slows once more, this time drastically, with a *molto rall.*, before picking up in the bars preceding Tempo I. Here (and in the coda which follows) right-hand ties need care while the inner voice projects the melodic line. A firm tone with no diminuendo or slackening of pace brings this section to an abrupt and dramatic stop. The coda then opens with three question-like reminiscences of the opening material at different dynamic levels, each one slower than its neighbour, giving time for reflection in the rests. A well-paced crescendo with prominent accents and some pedal creates excitement for the final build-up, and an allargando rounds off proceedings firmly and conclusively.

C:4 R. Nathaniel Dett *Honey*

This little-known love song, in turns capricious and heartfelt, will suit any player with a sentimental streak. An ability to go with the flow of the music is vital here; the player must make a wholehearted response to changes of mood.

The suggested brisk metronome mark of crotchet = 100 may be tempered to allow the opening to unfold gently. Very quiet tone and rhythmic freedom will capture the light-hearted, tender mood. The licence to place the right hand before the left at the tied acciaccaturas suggests an outdated way of playing expressively. Judicious use of pedal is needed here and elsewhere to sustain the harmonies without blurring the right hand's lines. Time seems almost suspended at the pause in bar 4 before impetus is regained to complete the phrase; the rhythm in bar 5 will need precise execution. Placing the left thumb on the G at the end of bar 7 removes the need for pedal. Bar 9 sees a meltingly beautiful upward shift to A minor and although the music is almost identical in pattern to that of the opening the sentiment seems heightened and more tender. A shapely melodic line is needed to convey the *molto espressivo* of bars 17–20, and the player may linger as if unwilling to let go of this moment of passion. Left-hand practice will help to synchronize the leaps and pedal changes at this point.

The *molto meno mosso* at bar 29 forms the central, most impassioned section of the piece – at this point, one can almost picture the lover fervently declaring his love on bended knee. *Parlando* and *recitando* suggest the flexibility of speech, although long notes must be held for their full length. Arm weight with a flexible wrist will produce a sonorous, non-percussive tone, and melodic notes should be well to the fore, with accents being treated as expressive, almost pleading, gestures. Clean pedal changes are required here, with care taken in the left hand to catch the fifth-finger notes in the widely spaced chords at bars 34 and 36.

Teneramente, a term often associated with Brahms, invites the player to indulge in the utmost tenderness and intimacy while enjoying the delicious harmonic shifts in the left hand. However it is important to re-establish tempo after each *rit.* In bars 41–4 a clear differentiation of dynamic level is needed to communicate the echoes. The biggest surprise of all occurs in the final four bars where the lover seems to dash off briskly, leaving the listener and probably also his sweetheart wondering whether he was serious after all!

C:5 Janáček *Our Evenings*

This piece may provide an introduction to the enigmatic style of one of the most original voices of early-twentieth-century music. Janáček's reputation rests mainly on orchestral music and operas: here one can sense vivid orchestral textures being conveyed through the medium of the piano.

The basic tonality oscillates between C sharp minor and major, enharmonically notated midway, but nothing is ever clear-cut with this elusive composer. Bar 15 to the change of signature is easier to grasp if one thinks of the accidentals producing the key of C sharp major. Some redistribution between the hands, as indicated, is needed at times, and smaller hands may resort to spreading the occasional chord. Although repeats are an integral part of Janáček's style they are not required for examination purposes.

The suggested crotchet = 80 works well as a tempo for the beginning and end but some relaxation of speed is necessary for the Adagio at bar 98. The irregular structure of the first section, with its characteristically contrasting long and repeated short phrases, can be conveyed by some rhythmic ebb and flow which allows the music to breathe as if sung. Here the harmonies and song-like melody contain all the soulful longing of Janáček's native land while the viola-like quaver line shared by both hands weaves sinuously through the texture. Pedalling beyond the occasional 'dab' indicated is necessary for producing a smooth line, but care should be taken not to create unwanted clashes with the scalic quaver line.

The switch to five flats heralds a change of mood as the woodwind-like semiquavers firstly decorate the melody then contribute to a powerful *fortissimo* climax at bar 64. The melodic line at bar 43 must project even at a very quiet dynamic level as it switches between hands; there can be a natural gathering of speed before applying the brakes at the accented notes.

Peace and serenity pervade the Adagio in which the treble and bass lines are given impetus by a gently repeating inner line. Thinking horizontally through phrases is vital to produce long phrases of two, eight-bar units followed by one of twelve bars. Although careful balance is needed to ensure that the semiquavers do not overpower the melody, they play their part in shaping the rise and fall of the lines. A return to the original tempo sees an abridged reference to the opening and the piece seems to fade into the distance as the tonality settles on a C sharp major chord.

C:6 Turina *Fiesta*

The word 'fiesta' conjures up a celebration, sometimes with a religious overtone or, in this case, simply party time! Excitement abounds as people dance and sing to guitars, yet there is also an air of tenderness and mystery in the quieter moments.

Although flexibility is needed in the smoother 'vocal' passages, a strong overall rhythmic drive should underpin any performance. *Allegro vivo* indicates a lively tempo (dotted crotchet = 132 seems good) but choice of speed will also be governed by the athletic passages, e.g. bars 43–6, and repeated notes and chords.

The ambiguity of the main key centres of A major and minor seems to evoke the Orient, a feature often present in Spanish music. Although notes should not present any major problems, the hand distribution in bars 27–34 and 51–4 demands care and attention. The B♯ in bar 14 might easily be missed, and close inspection will reveal that bars 39–43 form a recurring three-beat pattern. Changing fingers on repeated notes, as indicated, will help clarity of articulation (bar 45 may be fingered the same as bar 46 if 3-4-5 proves troublesome), and the light repeated chords at bar 11 need a hand-touch moving from the wrist.

Light quavers at the opening with buoyant, detached dotted crotchets will immediately establish the vivacious mood, and the *sforzando* in bar 9 can be highlighted by using a touch of pedal. The left-hand crotchets of the vamp-like figure in bars 11–14 need slight prominence and full length. A slight relaxation of impetus at bars 15–18, with tied notes not cut short, will allow time to enjoy the haunting *8ve* texture and major/minor contrasts. Similarly the sinuous right-hand melody at bar 23 invites a little rhythmic freedom.

Sufficient tone is needed to sustain the tied note at bar 27 over quieter chords, and an air of mystery is added if the dynamic level remains subdued until the steep crescendo at bar 34. The brilliance of a Spanish sun-lit day can be conveyed in the following E♭ section if the tone is confident and vibrant. Bars 39–46 ideally need memorizing in order for the player to concentrate on the keyboard. It is important to anticipate the left-hand downward shifts here, and the right hand's ascending quavers can be practised in block chords with the thumb on C♯; in performance the pedal will add colour and resonance to bars 43–6. No ritardando is needed at the ending, and the final chord will have full impact if the previous bars are kept *pianissimo*.